"*Why Liberty* showcases work by leading figures in Students For Liberty, the world's most dynamic youth movement for liberty, along with essays by venerable freedom fighters such as Tom Palmer and John Stossell. Fresh and new, tried and true, *Why Liberty* gives us hope for the next generation."

—John Tomasi,
Department of Political Science, Brown University

"This collection of essays is so informative and so well written that it will feed your desire to read more—and to know more—about the fundamental role of liberty in social order."

—Lynne Kiesling,
Department of Economics, Northwestern University

"This book is easy to read, good to read, and important to read. If more people read it, the world will be a much better place; there would be no need for the 'Why' in *Why Liberty*."

—Peter Kurrild-Klitgaard,
Department of Political Science, University of Copenhagen

"An inspiring guide that will benefit both those new to libertarianism and those well versed in the tradition. Though we often don't realise it, libertarianism is the principle by which most people lead their daily lives. This book explains why we should apply that principle to our politics, as well."

—Mark Pennington,
Department of Political Economy and Public Policy,
King's College, University of London

WHY LIBERTY

WHY LIBERTY

Your Life · Your Choices · Your Future

Edited by Tom G. Palmer

Students For Liberty
Atlas Network

JAMESON BOOKS, INC.

Ottawa, Illinois

AtlasNetwork.org   StudentsForLiberty.org

Published by Students For Liberty & Atlas Network / Jameson Books, Inc.

Edited by Tom G. Palmer
Cover Design by Jon Meyer

The editor gratefully acknowledges the assistance in preparing this book,
not only of the authors and copyright holders, but of the members of
Students For Liberty, most especially Clark Ruper and Matthew LaCorte,
who worked tirelessly to format and prepare the essays for publication.
Their dedication and zeal for liberty is itself an inspiration.

For information and other requests please write:

Students For Liberty, PO Box 17321, Arlington, VA 22216

The Atlas Network, 1201 L Street, NW, Washington, DC 20005

Jameson Books, Inc., 722 Columbus Street, PO Box 738, Ottawa, IL 61350
800-426-1357

Printed in the United States of America.

ISBN: 978-0-89803-172-0

16   15   14   13   5   4   3   2   1

CONTENTS

PREFACE

Politics is surely an important part of human life. After all, it's certainly one of the most hotly debated topics among all the things about which people argue. More people argue more excitedly about politics than just about anything else, not because it's inherently of greater interest than art or sports or chemistry or movies or architecture or medicine, but because it's about exercising power over other people.

When one solution gets imposed on everyone, a lot of people are likely to take a strong interest in what that solution is. If you don't want to be forced to do something by others, whether a party, a politician, or a government, you're likely to fight about it. And if you want to force others to do your bidding, the same applies.

Food would be as hotly debated as politics if all choices were made collectively and we were always doomed to get what everyone else got. Imagine the angry debates, coalitions, maneuvering, and scheming among and between gourmet "foodies" and fast food junkies, vegetarians and carnivores, weight lifters and weight watchers, if we were all limited to the same food, in the same portions. The same goes for other things people care about.

The ideas presented in this book are about an alternative view of politics: a politics not of force, but of persuasion, of live and let live, of rejecting both subjugation and domination. The essays are mainly written by younger people who are active in Students For Liberty, a very dynamic and exciting international movement. They reflect no narrow national perspective, but speak to the broad range of human experience. They offer an introduction to the philosophy by which most human beings live their lives on a day-to-day basis. That philosophy goes by various names around the world, including liberalism, classical liberalism (to distinguish it from what is called "liberalism" in the United States), and libertarianism. It's an approach that is at once simple and complicated, because it incorporates the insight that *simple rules* can generate *complex orders*. That's one of the most important lessons of modern social science. Order can emerge spontaneously, a topic that is explored in greater detail in this book's essays.

This short book is an invitation to think about important problems in new ways. It's for those who come to the issues for the first time and for advanced scholars. I hope that both groups and all in between will benefit from these essays. They can be read in any order and no chapter requires that one read another. A reader can "dip into" the book without having to read the whole thing. Think of it as a bag of healthy and tasty snacks for the mind. And enjoy.

Tom G. Palmer
Vilnius, Lithuania
June 3, 2013

1

WHY BE LIBERTARIAN?

By Tom G. Palmer

In a book titled Why Liberty, *it makes sense to dive right in with a straightforward explanation of what libertarianism is about and why people should embrace liberty as a principle of social order.*

As you go through life, chances are almost 100 percent that you act like a libertarian. You might ask what it means to "act like a libertarian." It's not that complicated. You don't hit other people when their behavior displeases you. You don't take their stuff. You don't lie to them to trick them into letting you take their stuff, or defraud them, or knowingly give them directions that cause them to drive off a bridge. You're just not that kind of person.

You respect other people. You respect their rights. You might sometimes feel like smacking someone in the face for saying something really offensive, but your better judgment prevails and you walk away, or answer words with words. You're a civilized person.

Congratulations. You've internalized the basic principles of libertarianism. You live your life and exercise your own freedom with respect for the freedom and rights of others. You behave as a libertarian.

Libertarians believe in the voluntary principle, rather than force. And more than likely, you do follow that principle in your everyday dealings with other people.

But hold on, isn't libertarianism a *political philosophy*, a set of ideas about government and policy? It is. So why isn't it rooted in what *government* should be doing, rather than in what individuals should be doing? Ah, here's the major difference between libertarianism and other ideas about politics. Libertarians don't believe that government is magical. It's made up of people. They're just like us. There's no special race of people—call them kings, emperors, wizards, Magi, presidents, legislators, or prime ministers—with super-normal intelligence, wisdom, or powers that elevate them above normal people. Rulers, even when democratically elected, are no more "public spirited," and sometimes far less, than average people. There's no evidence that they're any less selfish than other people or any more benevolent. And there's no evidence that they're more concerned with right or wrong than average people. They're like us.

But hold on again, political rulers *do* exercise powers that other people don't have. They exercise the powers to arrest people, to start wars and kill people, to decree what other people may or may not read, whether and how they may worship God, whom they may marry, what they may or may not eat, drink, or smoke, what they may or may not do for a living, where they may live, where they must attend school, whether they may travel, what goods and services they may provide to others and what prices they may charge, and a lot more. They certainly exercise powers the rest of us don't have.

Precisely. They wield force, and they do it as a matter of course—it's what distinguishes government from other institutions. But they have powers of perception, insight, or foresight no greater than the rest of us, nor standards of right and wrong that are higher or more rigorous than the average. Some may be smarter than average, others perhaps even less intelligent, but there's no evidence that they really exceed the rest of humanity in such a way that they should be considered elevated above us, as our natural masters.

Why do they exercise force, while the rest of us rely on

voluntary persuasion when we deal with others? The holders of political power aren't angels or gods, so why do they claim the authority to exercise powers that none among us would claim the right to exercise? Why should we submit to their exercise of force? If I have no authority to burst into your home to tell you what you should eat, or what you should smoke, or when you should go to bed, or with whom, why should a politician, or a bureaucrat, or an army general, or a king, or a governor have that authority?

Did We Consent to Be Coerced?

But wait, we *are* the government, aren't we? At least, in a democracy, as some clever philosophers, such as Jean-Jacques Rousseau, have argued, we consent to whatever the government tells us to do or not to do. The government carries out the "general will" of the people and that means that it's exercising our very own will. So when the government uses force against us, it's just forcing us to be free, by making us follow our own wills, and not what we happen to think we will. As Rousseau argued in his extraordinarily influential book *The Social Contract*, "the general will is always rightful and tends to the public good; but it does not follow that the deliberations of the people are always equally right. . . . There is often a great difference between the will of all [what all individuals want] and the general will."[1]

In his theory, Rousseau combined force with freedom, for, as he argued, "whoever refuses to obey the general will shall be constrained to do so by the whole body, which means nothing other than that he shall be forced to be free."[2] After all, you don't know what you *really* want until the state has decided what you want, so when you *think* you want to do something, but are stopped by the police and imprisoned, you're being made free. You were deluded into thinking you wanted to disobey the state, and the police are merely helping you to choose what you really wanted, but were too stupid, ignorant, foolish, or weak to know that you wanted.

Now that may be getting overly metaphysical, so let's dial back a bit and think about what is being argued by advocates of majority rule. Somehow, through elections or some other procedures, we generate the "will of the people," even though some of the people may not agree (at least the ones who lost the vote didn't agree with the majority). Those people will be coerced to go along with the majority, say, by not consuming alcohol or marijuana or by being made to give up their money to pay for things they oppose, such as foreign wars or subsidies to influential economic interests. A majority voted for the law banning X or requiring Y, or for candidates who pledged to ban X or require Y, and so now we know the "will of the people." And if someone still drinks a beer or smokes a joint or hides his or her income, that person is somehow not following the will of the people, to which he or she has consented. Let's unpack that a bit more.

Let's say a prohibitionist law was passed into effect and you had voted for the prohibitionist law or candidate. Some would say that you consented to be bound by the outcome. And if you voted against the prohibitionist law or for an antiprohibitionist candidate? Well, they would add, you participated in the procedure by which the decision was made, so you consented to be bound by the outcome. And if you didn't vote, or didn't even have an opinion? Well, they would add, you surely can't complain now, since you forfeited your chance to influence the outcome by not voting! As the English libertarian Herbert Spencer observed a long time ago of such arguments, "curiously enough, it seems that he gave his consent in whatever way he acted—whether he said yes, whether he said no, or whether he remained neuter! A rather awkward doctrine this."[3] Awkward, indeed. If you always "consent," regardless of what you actually say or do, then the term "consent" means nothing, because it means "non-consent," as well as "consent." When that is the case, a word has been emptied of meaning.

The fact is that a person who's arrested for smoking

marijuana in his or her own house didn't in any meaningful sense "consent" to being arrested. That's why the police carry sticks and guns—to threaten people with violence.

But maybe those powers are delegated to the government by the people, so if the people could choose not to smoke marijuana, then they could choose to arrest themselves. But if you don't have the authority to break down your neighbor's door and go in with guns drawn to drag them out and put them in a cage, how can you delegate that power to someone else? So we're back with the magical claim that your pot-smoking neighbors authorized their own arrest, regardless of what opinion they expressed, or how they behaved.

But maybe just being alive in a country means you've consented to everything the government demands of you. After all, if you come into my house, you certainly agree to be bound by my rules. But a "country" isn't quite like "my house." I own my house, but I don't "own" my country. It's made up of a lot of people who have their own ideas about how to live their lives. And they don't belong to me. That's really the most important realization of mature people: *other people don't belong to me.* They have their own lives to lead. You, as a mature person, understand that and your actions reflect it. You don't burst into the homes of others to tell them how to live. You don't steal their stuff when you think you have a better use for it. You don't hit, punch, stab, or shoot people when they disagree with you, even about matters of the greatest importance.

So, if you already *act like* a libertarian, maybe you should *be* one.

What Does It Mean to *Be* a Libertarian?

It means not only refraining from harming the rights of other people, namely, respecting the rules of justice with regards to other people, but also equipping yourself mentally to understand what it means for people to have rights, how rights create the foundation for peaceful social cooperation, and how voluntary societies work. It means standing up, not only for your own freedom, but for the freedom of other people. A great Brazilian thinker dedicated his life to the abolition of the greatest violation of liberty imaginable: slavery. His name was Joaquim Nabuco and he stated the libertarian creed that guided his own life:

> Educate your children, educate yourselves, in the love for the freedom of others, for only in this way will your own freedom not be a gratuitous gift from fate. You will be aware of its worth and will have the courage to defend it.[4]

Being a libertarian means caring about freedom for everyone. It means respecting the rights of other people, even when we find their actions or words disagreeable. It means refraining from the use of force and instead pursuing one's goals, whether personal happiness, or the improvement of the condition of humanity, or knowledge, or all of those, or something else, *exclusively* through voluntary and peaceful action, whether in the "capitalist" world of free enterprise and exchange, or in science, philanthropy, art, love, friendship, or any of the other human endeavors framed by the rules of voluntary cooperation.

Skepticism about Power and Authority

Being a libertarian means understanding that rights are secure only when power is limited. Rights require the rule of law. John Locke, the English radical philosopher and activist, helped to lay the foundations for the modern world. He argued against the advocates of "absolutism," those who believed that the rulers should exercise unlimited powers. Those who defended absolute power sneered that allowing people their "liberty" would mean everyone just doing whatever he or she "lists," that is, whatever he or she was inclined to do, as a matter of whim and without regard to consequences or the rights of others.

Locke responded that what the party of liberty sought was

"a Liberty to dispose, and order, as he lists, his Person, Actions, Possessions, and his whole Property, within the Allowance of those Laws under which he is; and therein not to be subject to the arbitrary Will of another, but freely follow his own."[5] One has the right to do whatever one chooses with what is one's own—to freely follow one's own will, rather than the commands of another, so long as one respects the equal rights of others.

The philosopher Michael Huemer grounds libertarianism in what he calls "common sense morality," which is comprised of three elements: "A nonaggression principle" that forbids individuals from attacking, killing, stealing from, or defrauding one another; "A recognition of the coercive nature of government . . . which is supported by credible threats of physical force directed against those who would disobey the state"; and "A skepticism of political authority . . . that the state may not do what it would be wrong for any nongovernmental person or organization to do."[6] As he notes, "it is the notion of *authority* that forms the true locus of dispute between libertarianism and other political philosophies."[7]

Liberty, Prosperity, and Order

Being a libertarian means understanding how wealth is created; not by politicians giving commands, but by free people working together, inventing, creating, saving, investing, buying and selling, all based on respect for the property, that is, the rights, of others. "Property" isn't limited just to "my stuff," as one might use the term today, but encompasses the rights to "Life, Liberty, and Estate," to use Locke's famous phrase.[8] As James Madison, the principal author of the US Constitution argued, "[A]s a man is said to have a right to his property, he may be equally said to have a property in his rights."[9]

Love and affection may be enough for small groups to cooperate peacefully and efficiently, but libertarians understand that they aren't sufficient to create peace and cooperation among large groups of people who don't interact face-to-face.

Libertarians believe in the rule of law, meaning rules that are applicable to everyone and not bent or stretched this way or that based on the preferences of people with power. The rules of free societies are not crafted to benefit this or that person or group; they respect the rights of every human being, regardless of gender, color, religion, language, family, or other accidental feature.

The rules of property are among the most important foundations for voluntary cooperation among strangers. Property isn't just what you can hold in your hands; it's the complex relationships of rights and obligations by which people who are unknown to each other can guide their actions and that allow them to live peacefully, to cooperate in firms and associations, and to trade for mutual advantage, because they know the baseline—what's mine and what's yours—from which each may act to improve his or her condition. Well-defined, legally secure, and transferrable property rights form the foundation for voluntary cooperation, widespread prosperity, progress, and peace.[10] That includes not only the things you can hold in your hand or stand on, but shares of complicated business enterprises that produce any of the uncountable things that require the cooperation of thousands and thousands of people, whether medicines or aircraft or pineapples delivered to your table in winter.

The libertarian law professor Richard Epstein titled one of his best books *Simple Rules for a Complex World*.[11] The title brilliantly captures his theme, that you don't need complex rules to generate complex forms of order. Simple rules will do. In fact, simple, understandable, and stable rules tend to generate order, whereas complicated, incomprehensible, and fluctuating rules tend to generate chaos.

Well-defined property and the right to trade on mutually agreeable terms make possible large-scale cooperation without coercion. Free markets incorporate more, not less, order and foresight than coercively directed or commanded societies. The spontaneous order of markets is far more abstract, complex, and farsighted than all the five-year plans or economic interventions ever devised. Institutions such as prices, which emerge when people are free to exchange, help to guide resources to their most highly valued uses, without vesting coercive power in a bureaucracy.[12] Coercively imposed "planning" is, in fact, the opposite of planning; it is a disruption of the continuous process of plan coordination embodied in freely developed social institutions.

Order emerges spontaneously from the free interactions of people who are secure in the enjoyment of their rights. That applies not only to economic order, but also to language, social mores, customs, science, and even fields such as fashion and style. To use force in the attempt to subject any or all of those areas to the arbitrary will of a ruler, a dictator, a president, a committee, a legislature, or a bureaucracy is to replace order with chaos, freedom with force, and harmony with discord.

Libertarians believe in and work for a world at peace, in which the rights of each and every unique human being are recognized and respected, a world in which widely shared prosperity is generated by voluntary cooperation, based on a legal system that protects rights and facilitates mutually beneficial exchanges. Libertarians believe in and work for limits on power, for the subjection of heretofore arbitrary power to the rule of law, for the limitation and minimization of violence of all sorts. Libertarians believe in and stand up for the freedom to think, to work, to behave in any way one chooses, so long as one respects the equal freedom of others. Libertarians believe in and work for a world in which each person is free to pursue her or his own happiness, without requiring anyone else's permission to be, to act, to live.

So . . . Why Be Libertarian?

Why be libertarian? It may sound glib, but a reasonable response is, Why not? Just as the burden of proof is on the one who accuses another of a crime, not on the one accused, the burden of proof is on the one who would deny liberty to another person, not the one who would exercise liberty. Someone who wishes to sing a song or bake a cake should not have to begin by begging permission from all the others in the world to be allowed to sing or bake. Nor should she or he have to rebut all possible reasons against singing or baking. If she is to be forbidden from singing or baking, the one who seeks to forbid should offer a good reason why she should not be allowed to do so. The burden of proof is on the forbidder. And it may be a burden that could be met, if, for example, the singing were to be so loud it would make it impossible for others to sleep or the baking would generate so many sparks it would burn down the homes of the neighbors. Those would be good reasons for forbidding the singing or the baking. The presumption, however, is for liberty, and not for the exercise of power to restrict liberty.

A libertarian is someone who believes in the presumption of liberty. And with that simple presumption, when realized in practice, comes a world in which different people can realize their own forms of happiness in their own ways, in which people can trade freely to mutual advantage, and disagreements are resolved with words, and not with clubs. It would not be a perfect world, but it would be a world worth fighting for.

2

THERE OUGHT *NOT* TO BE A LAW

By John Stossel

When people see a problem, they often reach for the easiest solution: pass a law. That doesn't always work out, because force rarely changes things for the better, and that's what those "laws" really are, just exercises of force. John Stossel started his investigative journalism career as a consumer reporter, worked for ABC News, was co-anchor of the television show 20/20, and now hosts the Stossel show at Fox Business News. His show, Stossel, has been filmed twice at the International Students For Liberty Conference with audiences of Students For Liberty members.

I'm a libertarian in part because I see a false choice offered by the political left and right: government control of the economy—or government control of our personal lives.

People on both sides think of themselves as freedom lovers. The left thinks government can lessen income inequality. The right thinks government can make Americans more virtuous. I say we're best off if neither side attempts to advance its agenda via government.

Let both *argue* about things like drug use and poverty, but let no one be coerced by government unless he steals or attacks someone. Beyond the small amount needed to fund a highly limited government, let no one forcibly take other people's money. When in doubt, leave it out—or rather, leave it to the market and other voluntary institutions.

But this is not how most people think. Most people see a world full of problems that can be solved by laws. They assume it's just the laziness, stupidity, or indifference of politicians that keeps them from solving our problems. But government is force—and inefficient.

That's why it's better if government didn't try to address most of life's problems.

People tend to believe that "government can!" When problems arise, they say, "There ought to be a law!"

Even the collapse of the Soviet Union, caused by the appalling results of central planning, didn't shock the world into abandoning big government. Europe began talking about some sort of "market socialism." Politicians in the United States dreamt of a "third way" between capitalism and socialism, and of "managed capitalism"—where politicians often replace the invisible hand.

George W. Bush ran for president promising a "lean" government, but he decided to create a $50 billion per year prescription drug entitlement and build a new bureaucracy called No Child Left Behind. Under Bush, Republicans *doubled* discretionary spending (the greatest increase since LBJ), expanded the drug war and hired 90,000 new regulators.

Bush's increases in regulation didn't mollify the media's demand for still more.

Then came Barack Obama and spending big enough to bankrupt all our children. That fueled the Tea Party and the 2010 elections.

The Tea Party gave me hope, but I was fooled again. Within months, the new "fiscally conservative" Republicans voted to preserve farm subsidies, vowed to "protect" Medicare, and cringed when Romney's future veep choice, Rep. Paul Ryan, proposed his mild deficit plan.

It is unfortunate that the United States, founded partly on libertarian principles, cannot admit that government has gotten too big. East Asian countries embraced markets and flourished. Sweden and Germany liberalized their labor markets and saw their economies improve.

But we keep passing new rules.

The enemy here is human intuition. Amid the dazzling bounty of the marketplace, it's easy to take the benefits of markets for granted. I can go to a foreign country and stick a piece of plastic in the wall, and cash will come out. I can give that same piece of plastic to a stranger who doesn't even speak my language—and he'll rent me a car for a week. When I get home, Visa or MasterCard will send me the accounting—correct to the penny. We take such things for granted.

Government, by contrast, can't even count votes accurately.

Yet whenever there are problems, people turn to government. Despite the central planners' long record of failure, few of us like to think that the government which sits atop us, taking credit for everything, could really be all that rotten.

The great twentieth-century libertarian H. L. Mencken lamented, "A government at bottom is nothing more than a group of men, and as a practical matter most of them are inferior men.... Yet these nonentities, by the intellectual laziness of men in general ... are generally obeyed as a matter of duty ... [and] assumed to have a kind of wisdom that is superior to ordinary wisdom."

There is nothing government can do that we cannot do better as free individuals—and as groups of individuals working freely together.

Without big government, our possibilities are limitless.

3

Libertarianism as Radical Centrism

By Clark Ruper

For many years it's been customary to think about a continuous spectrum of political thought, from "left" to "right." Does libertarianism fit on that spectrum as it is traditionally presented? Clark Ruper, vice president of Students For Liberty, suggests a new approach to thinking about the relationship among competing political ideas and how libertarianism provides the baseline for much contemporary discussion and debate. Ruper received his degree in history from the University of Michigan in Ann Arbor.

The left–right political spectrum is the standard introduction to political thought: if you believe X, you are on the left, and if you believe Y, you are on the right. What X and Y represent varies depending on with whom you speak; its invocation encourages people to place themselves someplace on that spectrum, even if their views don't locate them on one spot on that spectrum. It's made especially absurd when we're told that "the two extremes meet, making the spectrum into a circle," with rival forms of violent collectivism at each end. So when you first hear of classical liberalism or libertarianism, you may ask yourself on which side the philosophy falls on "the spectrum." It doesn't.

Inherent in the ideas of liberty is a rejection of the standard left–right spectrum. Libertarianism is an ideology that questions and challenges the use of political power. Instead of a choice between government intervention in this area or in that area, libertarianism sees politics as a struggle of liberty against power. Libertarians take very seriously the lesson of the historian Lord Acton: "Power tends to corrupt, and absolute power corrupts absolutely."[13] Libertarianism does not fall onto one side or another of a spectrum with advocates of one kind of coercive power or another on each side.

The traditional left–right spectrum shows communism on one end and fascism on the other, tobacco prohibition on one side and marijuana prohibition on the other, and speech codes on one side . . . and speech codes on the other. So which is coherent and which incoherent, libertarianism or the left–right spectrum? You can decide for yourself.

In a sense, if one were to insist on a linear spectrum, libertarians could be said to occupy the radical center of political discourse. Libertarians are radical in our analysis—we go to the root (Latin: *radix*) of the issues—and we believe in the principles of liberty. One could call us centrist in the sense that from the center we project our ideas outward and inform political parties and ideologies across the spectrum. As a result, libertarian ideas pervade both the center-left and the center-right, providing them with their most appealing qualities. Moreover, an increasing percentage of the citizens in many countries should be seen as libertarian, rather than as on the "left" or the "right."[14]

Libertarianism is a political philosophy centered on the importance of individual liberty. A libertarian can be "socially conservative" or "socially progressive," urban or rural, religious or not, a teetotaler or a drinker, married or single . . . you get the point. What unites libertarians is a consistent adherence to the presumption of liberty in human affairs, that, in the words of the Cato Institute's David Boaz, "It's the exercise of power, not the exercise of freedom, that requires justification."[15] Libertarians are consistent defenders of the principle of liberty and are able to work with a wide variety of people and groups on issues in which individual liberty, peace, and limited government are implicated.

The libertarian radical center has shaped much of the modern world. As journalist Fareed Zakaria observed:

> Classical liberalism, we are told, has passed from the scene. If so, its epitaph will read as does Sir Christopher Wren's, engraved on his monument at St. Paul's Cathedral: "Si monumentum requiris, circumspice." If you are searching for a monument, look around. Consider the world we live in—secular, scientific, democratic, middle class. Whether you like it or not, it is a world made by liberalism. Over the last two hundred years, liberalism (with its power ally, capitalism) has destroyed an order that had dominated human society for two millennia—that of authority, religion, custom, land, and kings. From its birthplace in Europe, liberalism spread to the United States and is now busily remaking most of Asia.[16]

Libertarianism (the contemporary name for principled classical liberalism) has already profoundly shaped the modern world. In much of the world, many battles have already been fought and in many places won: separation of church and state; limitation of power through constitutions; freedom of speech; debunking mercantilism and replacing it with free trade; abolition of slavery; personal freedom and legal toleration for minorities, whether religious, ethnic, linguistic, or sexual; protection of property; the defeat of fascism, Jim Crow, apartheid, National Socialism, and communism. Far too many intellectuals and activists to name made those victories possible, but they made the world better—more just, more peaceful, and more free. They made the libertarian position on those and many other issues the baseline for reasonable political discourse. But we are not content to rest on our laurels. As always, old battles must often be fought again. And, for the youth of today, as was the case for preceding generations, there remain many battles to fight and freedoms to win.

How have libertarians managed such influence while operating largely outside of the party structure? Sometimes we do form our own parties, as evidenced by the various (classical) liberal parties in Europe and other countries today. Sometimes we work within minor parties, as with the Libertarian Party in the United States, whose 2012 presidential candidate, Governor Gary Johnson, educated millions about the harm caused by the war on drugs and other government programs. Sometimes we work within existing party structures, exemplified by Ron Paul's presidential campaigns as a Republican in 2008 and 2012. He was able to advance many libertarian principles by using the soap box of a political campaign to reach thousands of young people, not only in the United States, but around the world. While our political activism takes many forms depending on the country and the context, our ideas inform the political spectrum.

Consider 1960s America, regarded as the golden age of radical student activism in the United States. On the right you had the conservative Young Americans for Freedom (YAF). Their founding Sharon Statement, which was adopted in 1960, claimed, "That liberty is indivisible, and that political freedom cannot long exist without economic freedom; That the purpose of government is to protect those freedoms through the preservation of internal order, the provision of national defense, and the administration of justice; That when government ventures beyond these rightful functions, it accumulates power, which tends to diminish order and liberty;"[17] Their hero, Senator Barry Goldwater, in his address to the nation, stated, "I would remind you that extremism in the defense of liberty is no vice. And let me remind you also that moderation in the pursuit of justice is no virtue."[18]

At the same time, the Students for a Democratic Society (SDS) was emerging on the left as leaders of the anti-war movement. In their Port Huron Statement, which was adopted in 1962, they affirmed: "We regard men as infinitely precious and possessed of unfulfilled capacities for reason, freedom, and love. The decline of utopia and hope is in fact one of the defining features of social life today. The reasons are various: the dreams of the older left were perverted by Stalinism and never recreated . . . the horrors of the twentieth century, symbolized in the gas-ovens and concentration camps and atom bombs, have blasted hopefulness. To be idealistic is to be considered apocalyptic, deluded."[19]

Former SDS President Carl Ogelsby recalled in his memoir, *Ravens in the Storm*, "Libertarianism is a stance that allows one to speak to the right as well as the left, which is what I was always trying to do . . . Why go to rightists on this theme when there were so many leftists to choose from? Because you made the strongest case against the war if you could show that both right and left oppose it."[20] Moreover, "I had decided early on that it made sense to speak of 'the radical center' and 'militant moderation.' I meant that we should be radical in our analysis but centrist in reaching out to conservatives."[21]

While they varied in their areas of emphasis—YAF on economic freedom and opposition to socialism; SDS on civil rights and peace—taken as a whole they can be regarded as pioneers of libertarian activism in the modern age. The leaders of those movements went on to become the teachers, journalists, professors, politicians, and other figures who drive the public discourse today. They claimed allegiance to the left and the right, but their best intellectual arguments and energy came from their underlying libertarian impulses.

The war on drugs is increasingly being acknowledged as a disaster. Libertarian think tanks such as the Cato Institute have documented for decades the deadly costs of the drug war and the benefits of personal responsibility and personal liberty. Libertarian economists, notably including Milton Friedman, have explained the perverse incentives created by prohibition.[22] Moral philosophers have argued that a society of free and responsible individuals would eliminate prohibitions on victimless crimes, going back to Lysander Spooner's 1875 pamphlet, *Vices Are Not Crimes: A Vindication of Moral Liberty*.[23] Because libertarians blazed the trail by pointing out the harmful effects of prohibition—on morality, on justice, on crime rates, on families, on social order—more and more political leaders are speaking out about the disastrous consequences of the war on drugs without fear of being smeared as "pro-drugs." They include presidents of Mexico, Guatemala, Colombia, and Brazil, countries that have suffered from the crime, the violence, and the corruption brought by prohibition, as well as governors, former secretaries of state, judges, police chiefs, and many others.[24]

What makes libertarians unique is that while others may hold particular pro-liberty beliefs casually or on an ad hoc basis, libertarians advocate them from principle. Libertarianism is not a philosophy of the right or of the left. It is the radical center, the home for those who wish to live and let live, who cherish both their own freedom and the freedom of others, who reject the stale clichés and false promises of collectivism, both "on the left" and "on the right."

Where on the left–right spectrum does libertarianism stand? Above it.

4

The History and Structure of Libertarian Thought

By Tom G. Palmer

History can help to show how ideas emerge and how they relate to each other. The idea of liberty is examined historically and conceptually to show how libertarian thought presents a coherent understanding of the world and how humans should treat each other.

Although elements of libertarian thought can be found throughout human history, libertarianism as a political philosophy appeared with the modern age. It is the modern philosophy of individual freedom, rather than serfdom or subservience; of legal systems based on the enjoyment of rights, rather than the exercise of arbitrary power; of mutual prosperity through free labor, voluntary cooperation, and exchange, rather than forced labor, compulsion, and the exploitation of the plundered by their conquerors; and of toleration and mutual co-existence of religions, lifestyles, ethnic groups, and other forms of human existence, rather than religious, tribal, or ethnic warfare. It is the philosophy of the modern world and it is rapidly spreading among young people around the globe.

To understand the growing worldwide libertarian movement, one needs to understand the ideas that constitute the political philosophy of libertarianism. One can understand political philosophies in a variety of ways. One can study them historically to see how they came together as a response to a set of problems or issues. Ideas are in some ways like tools—mental tools that help us interact with each other and the world. To understand such tools better, it helps to know the problems to which they are presented as solutions. Historical study helps us to understand ideas. One can also understand their logical relations, that is, the ways in which the various concepts or ideas—such as justice, rights, law, freedom, and order—interact and give meaning to each other.[25] This short essay offers a short introduction to both ways of understanding libertarianism.

Libertarianism Understood Historically

Looked at historically, libertarianism is the modern form of a movement that was once known as liberalism. That term, "liberalism," especially in the United States, has lost some of its earlier meaning. As the famous economist Joseph Schumpeter noted, "as a supreme, if unintended, compliment, the enemies of the system of private enterprise have thought it wise to appropriate its label."[26] The term liberalism or its variants are still used in much of the rest of the world, however, for what is now called libertarianism or "classical liberalism" in the US. Because of the confusion of terms in the US, many people have adopted the term libertarianism, which shares the common Latin root for liberty, to distinguish their views from what is typically called "liberalism" in the US. The term is sometimes also used to distinguish more thoroughly consistent forms of liberalism from more pragmatic or flexible forms of liberalism. (In other languages the same word is used to translate both liberalism and libertarianism; Hungarian, for example, uses both szabadelvűség and liberalizmus for liberalism/libertarianism.)

So where did liberalism come from? Liberalism emerged in Europe and other regions of the world as a defense of a new way of living together on the basis of peace, toleration, and mutually beneficial voluntary exchange and cooperation. Liberalism offered a defense of such peaceful forms of life against the doctrines of the absolute and all-powerful state, known as "absolutism." In the course of debates over the proper extent and scope of power, the ideas of liberalism became sharper, more radical, and mutually reinforcing.

Trade and commerce began to increase in Europe following the Dark Ages, especially due to the growth of independent "communes," or self-governing cities, often protected from pirates, raiders, and warlords by thick walls.[27] New cities—places of production and trade—were being founded throughout Europe. The new cities and their "civil societies" were known as places of personal freedom, as expressed in the old German slogan "*Stadtluft macht frei*" ("City air makes one free"), and peace.[28]

As one historian noted, "Without liberty, that is to say, without the power to come and go, to do business, to sell goods, a power not enjoyed by serfdom, trade was impossible."[29] Civil (from *civitas*, city) society refers to the societies that emerged in such cities. Very importantly, the term also came to denote a way of treating each other: civil behavior. Being civil means being polite to strangers, being honest in one's dealings, and respecting the rights of others. Such new cities and associations were characterized by various kinds of representative or popular assemblies that deliberated about laws and public policies. Associated with civil society was the new idea of "civil rights," meaning the rights necessary for a civil society.

As trade grew and more wealth was accumulated, kings began to create modern military systems, which they used to extend their power over both the feudal aristocracy, whose power generally had the same roots in violent conquest as the power of kings, and over the cities, which were rooted in voluntary association. The "military revolution" concentrated more and more power in what was to become known later as "the state," typically in the person and powers of the king.[30]

Such centralized and monarchical political systems displaced, conquered, and assimilated most of the other political systems that had characterized Europe, including independent "city-states," the Hanseatic League of merchant cities, the Holy Roman Empire, and other forms of political association. As such "sovereigns" grew in power, they claimed to be "above the law" and to exercise absolute power over all other forms of human association.[31] Increasingly, kings asserted that they had the "divine right" to exercise absolute power. The secular powers and the religious hierarchies formed alliances, often with the secular powers dominating the religious, but sometimes the other way around, with the latter known as theocratic rule.

The doctrine of absolutism held that the ruler was above the law, which was a major break with the prior tradition that the law, not personal power, was supreme. King James VI and I, as he was known (King James VI of Scotland who became also King James I of England in 1603), stated in 1598, "the King is over-Lord of the whole land; so he is Master over every person that inhabiteth the same, having power over the life and death of every one of them. For although a just Prince will not take the life of any of his subjects without a cleare law, yet the same lawes whereby he taketh them, are made by himselfe, or his predecessours, and so the power flowes always from him selfe . . . I have at length proved, that the King is above the law, as both the author and giver of strength thereto."[32]

Absolutism had an economic theory to accompany it: mercantilism, the idea that the king and his bureaucracies should direct industry, forbid this enterprise and subsidize that one, grant monopolies to favored companies (a practice now referred to as cronyism), "protect" the owners of local industries against competition from lower priced imported goods, and generally manage trade to the benefit of the ruling powers of the state, with the aim of bringing money into the state's treasury.[33]

Liberalism emerged as a defense of the freedom of civil society against the claims of absolute power, against monopolies and privileges, mercantilism, protectionism, war, and public debt, and in favor of civil rights and the rule of law. That movement drew on many sources. Prominent among them were the ideas of individual rights articulated by the Spanish Scholastic thinkers of Salamanca, who defended both the market economy and the rights of the conquered Indians against their rapacious Spanish overlords, as well as the doctrines of natural law and natural rights articulated by Dutch and German thinkers, but arguably the first fully libertarian movement emerged during the civil wars in England: the Levellers.[34] The Levellers fought on the parliamentary side in the English Civil War (1642–1651) for limited, constitutional government, for freedom of religion, for freedom of trade, for protection of property, for the right to earn a living, for equal rights for all. They were radicals, abolitionists, and human rights and peace advocates. They were libertarians.

Those ideas—of individual rights, of limited government, of freedom of thought, religion, speech, trade, production, and travel—opened minds, shattered ancient bonds, generated unprecedented wealth for the average person, and brought down one empire after another. Slavery was brought to an end in Europe, in North America, and in South America, culminating in abolition of slavery in Brazil on May 13, 1888. Feudalism was eliminated. The serfs of Europe were liberated, sometimes all at once, sometimes in stages: Austria in 1781 and 1848; Denmark in 1788; Serbia in 1804 and 1830; Bavaria in 1808; Hungary and Croatia in 1848; Russia in 1861 and 1866; and Bosnia and Herzegovina in 1918.

The movement for liberty grew not only throughout Europe and Europe's colonies, but spread through the Islamic world, China, and elsewhere, drawing on local traditions of liberty. For libertarian ideas are not the product of only one culture; every culture and every tradition has a narrative of liberty, as well as a narrative of power. Europe produced Voltaire and Adam Smith, but also later Mussolini, Lenin, and Hitler. Marx, whose doctrines dominated China for decades, was not Chinese, but German. Libertarian sages and voices can be found in every culture, as can the advocates of absolute power. Libertarianism is taking root worldwide, connecting with local libertarian traditions, especially in Africa and in Asia, as well as rediscovering connections in Europe, Latin America, and North America.

The contemporary libertarian movement builds not only on the experience of earlier liberals in combating absolutism, but also on the experience of the horrors of an even more malignant threat to liberty and civilization: collectivist totalitarianism. In the nineteenth century the tide of libertarian thought started to crest. New political ideologies, drawing on the older traditions of power, emerged to challenge liberalism. Imperialism, racism, socialism, nationalism, communism, fascism, and all their combinations, all rested on the fundamental premises of collectivism. The individual was not seen as the repository of rights; what mattered, they asserted, was the rights and interests of the nation, the class, or the race, all expressed through the power of the state.

By 1900 the libertarian editor of *The Nation*, E. L. Godkin, wrote in a depressing editorial, "Only a remnant, old men for the most part, still uphold the Liberal doctrine, and when they are gone, it will have no champions." More chillingly, he predicted the horrifying collectivist oppression and war that would cost hundreds of millions their lives in the coming century: "We hear no more of natural rights, but of inferior races, whose part it is to submit to the government of those whom God has made their superiors. The old fallacy of divine right has once more asserted its ruinous power, and before it is again repudiated there must be international struggles on a terrific scale."[35] And so it turned out to be. The consequence was mass murder on a scale never seen before, systems of mass enslavement on a new scale, and world wars that ravaged

Europe, Eurasia, Asia, and which had terrible spillovers in South America, Africa, and the Middle East.[36]

The challenge posed to liberty, to civilization, to life itself by collectivism dramatically shaped the libertarian response. That included a renewed emphasis on the following elements of libertarian thought, all of which had been denied by collectivist ideologies such as socialism, communism, National Socialism, and fascism:

- The primacy of the individual human being as the fundamental moral unit, rather than the collective, whether state, class, race, or nation;
- Individualism and the right of every human being to pursue his or her own happiness in his or her own way;
- Property rights and the market economy as a decentralized and peaceful means of decision making and coordination that effectively utilizes the knowledge of millions or billions of people;
- The importance of the voluntary associations of civil society, including family, religious community, neighborhood association, business firm, labor union, friendly society, professional association, and myriad others that provide meaning and substance to life and help individuals to achieve their unique identities through their multiple affiliations, and which are displaced by expansions of state power;
- A fear of the state and of concentrations of power in the military and in the executive organs of state power.

Many persons contributed to the revival of libertarian thought, especially after World War II was winding to a close. In 1943 three books were published in the United States that returned libertarian ideas to popular discussion: Rose Wilder Lane's *The Discovery of Freedom*, Isabel Paterson's *The God of the*

Machine, and Ayn Rand's runaway bestseller *The Fountainhead*. In 1944 in the United States Ludwig von Mises issued his book *Omnipotent Government: The Rise of the Total State and Total War*, and in the United Kingdom F. A. Hayek issued his bestselling challenge to collectivist economic planning, *The Road to Serfdom*. Hayek's book was then released in other countries to great acclaim. Hayek also organized the Mont Pelerin Society, an international society of classical liberal scholars which held its first meeting in 1947 in Switzerland. More books appeared, as did societies, associations, publishing houses, think tanks, student clubs, political parties, and far more.[37]

Think tanks to promote classical liberal ideas were started. The first wave was in the 1940s and 1950s, with such still vigorous organizations as the Institute for Public Affairs in Australia (1943), the Foundation for Economic Education in the US (1946), and the Institute of Economic Affairs in the UK (1955). The Cato Institute was founded in the US in 1977 and Timbro was founded in Sweden in 1978, as a part of a second wave of libertarian think tanks that has changed discussions about public policy. (Hundreds have since followed and most are affiliated with the Atlas Network, which was founded by Sir Antony Fisher, also the founder of the Institute of Economic Affairs.) Eminent intellectuals followed in the footsteps of Paterson, Lane, Rand, Mises, and Hayek, such as philosophers Robert Nozick, H. B. Acton, and Antony Flew, and Nobel Prize–winning economists James Buchanan, Milton Friedman, Ronald Coase, George Stigler, Robert Mundell, Elinor Ostrom, and Vernon Smith, to name a few, who advanced libertarian arguments and applied libertarian ideas to a wide array of social, economic, legal, and political problems.

As libertarian ideas gain more adherents and champions throughout the Middle East, Africa, Asia, Latin America, and the countries of the former Soviet Union, libertarianism is again adapting to new problems, notably the need to build and strengthen the institutions of civil society and to do so on the basis of traditions indigenous to those societies. Such needed institutions include habits of peaceful discussion, rather than violence; mutual respect for persons regardless of gender, race, religion, sexuality, or language; independent judicial systems to adjudicate disputes peacefully; systems of property rights that are well defined, legally secure, and easily transferable, to facilitate wealth creating exchanges; freedom of the press and public discussion; and traditions and institutions to check the exercise of power.

So much for a brief summation of the history of libertarianism. Let's turn now to another way to understand libertarianism.

Libertarianism Understood Conceptually: The Libertarian Tripod

A chair with just one leg will fall over. Add another and it's marginally more stable, but it will still fall over. Add a third to make a tripod and each will reinforce the others. Ideas can be like that, too. Ideas—about rights, justice, social order, law—don't just stand on their own. They fill out each other's meaning. Like the legs of a tripod, they lend support to each other.

Libertarianism is based on the fundamental ideal of liberty; libertarians hold liberty to be the highest *political* value. That doesn't mean that liberty must be the highest value in life; after all, people fall in love, pursue truth and beauty, and have ideas on religion and many other important matters, and politics is certainly not the only thing that matters in life. But for libertarians, the primary value to be realized in politics is liberty. Political life is about securing justice and peace and shared prosperity, and libertarians draw on a long tradition of classical liberal thought that sees those principles and values as mutually reinforcing.

The libertarian tripod is made up of three pillars:

Individual Rights: individuals have rights that are prior to political association; those rights are not dispensations from power, but can be exerted even against power; as Nozick began his libertarian classic *Anarchy, State, and*

Utopia, "Individuals have rights, and there are things no person or group may do to them (without violating their rights)."[38]

Spontaneous Order: it is common for people to assume that all order must be the product of an ordering mind, but the most important kinds of order in society are not the results of conscious planning or design, but emerge from the voluntary interaction and mutual adjustments of plans of free persons acting on the basis of their rights;

Constitutionally Limited Government: rights require protection by institutions that are empowered to use force in their defense, but those same institutions often represent the greatest and most dangerous threat to rights, meaning that they must be strictly limited through constitutional mechanisms, including divisions of and competition among sources of power, legal systems that are independent of executive power, and widely shared insistence on the supremacy of law over power.

Each of the above pillars gives support to the others. Rights must be clearly defined and protected by institutions of law; when rights are well defined and legally secure, order will emerge spontaneously; when social order and harmony emerges without planned direction, people are more likely to respect the rights of others; when people are accustomed to exercising their rights and respecting the rights of others, they are more likely to insist on constitutional restraints on legal institutions.

Individual Rights

Libertarian ideas about rights were forged largely in the struggle for religious freedom and for the freedom of the weak who suffered oppression from the strong. The Spanish thinker Francisco de Vitoria, in his famous book of 1539 on the American Indians, defended the indigenous people of the Americas against the brutality and oppression brought by the

Spanish Empire. He argued that the Indians had moral responsibility for their actions ("dominium") and concluded that,

> the barbarians [the term used at the time for non-European and non-Christian peoples] undoubtedly possessed as true dominion, both public and private as any Christian. That is to say, they could not be robbed of their property, either as private citizens or as princes, on the grounds that they were not true masters (*ueri domini*).[39]

The Indians, argued Vitoria and his followers, were as entitled to respect for their lives, their property, and their countries as any Spaniard. They had rights and to violate them was an injustice that should be resisted. The ideas of moral responsibility and rights had an enormous impact on thinking generally about human beings; it was not the accident of birth that mattered, but whether one was a moral agent, a being who could be held responsible for his or her choices and actions.

At about the same time, the defenders of freedom of religion insisted, and often paid with their lives for doing so, that because human beings were responsible beings capable of thought, deliberation, and choice, conscience must be free and that religion should be a matter of choice, and not of compulsion. The right to freedom of religion was a right, not a privilege conferred by those with power. The theologian John Calvin had defended the murder in Geneva of his critic Servetus for preaching a different understanding of the gospel, on the grounds that the rulers were obliged to defend the true faith. The great sixteenth-century champion of religious liberty Sebastian Castellio responded directly to Calvin: "To kill a man is not to defend a doctrine, it is to kill a man. When the Genevans killed Servetus, they did not defend a doctrine, they killed a man."[40] A doctrine should be defended with words to change the mind and heart, not weapons and fire to break and burn the body of the one who disagrees. As the English poet John Milton noted in his path-breaking argument for freedom of the press, *Areopagetica*, "here the great art lies to discern in what the law is to bid restraint and punishment, and in what things persuasion only is to work."[41]

Those early pioneers of liberty who insisted on respect for equal rights, regardless of religion, race, gender, or other accidental features of persons were met with a powerful challenge from the advocates of absolutist or theocratic rule, who responded that if each person had the right to manage his or her own life, there would be no overall plan for society, and thus chaos and disorder would ensue. There has to be a boss, the absolutists and theocrats said, someone with the power to envision and then impose order on a disorderly mass. Otherwise, you wouldn't know what to produce, or what to do with it, or how to worship God, or what to wear, or how much to spend or save.

Spontaneous Order

By itself, the moral principle of respect for persons was unable to meet that challenge, until social scientists began to unlock the secrets of complex orders. Just as modern entomologists have discovered that the complex order of a bee hive is not "ruled" by a queen exercising absolute power and issuing commands to the other bees, as was widely believed for millennia, even earlier social scientists discovered that complex human societies are not "ruled" by any humans with such powers, telling dairy farmers when to milk the cows and how much to charge for the milk, setting the value of money, and authoritatively issuing orders to realize the order of society generally. Instead, as they learned, if you want an orderly and prosperous society, one should rely on the maxim *"Laissez faire et laissez passer, le monde va de lui même!"* as it was phrased by the early libertarian intellectual Jacques Claude Marie Vincent de Gournay in the eighteenth century.[42]

Complex orders cannot simply be commanded. Language,

the market economy, common law, and many other complex forms of coordination among persons unknown to each other emerge, not through coercive imposition of a plan that emerges from the mind of a great leader (or the minds of a committee of them), but as byproducts of the interaction of people following relatively simple rules, much as flocks of birds, schools of fish, and hives of bees exhibit complex forms of order without a directing mind.

It's not an easy thing to grasp. When we see an ordered set of things, we tend to look around for the order-er. If I see a well-arranged row of chairs, I would probably ask, "Who put all the chairs in order?" But most order, including the order of the market economy, is, as the Nobel Laureate in Economics James Buchanan argued, defined in the process of its emergence: "the 'order' of the market emerges only from the process of voluntary exchange among the participating individuals. The 'order' is, itself, defined as the outcome of the process that generates it. The 'it,' the allocation-distribution result, does not, and cannot, exist independently of the trading process. Absent this process, there is and can be no 'order.'"[43] That's not easy for the human mind to grasp, because we seem predisposed to look for creators of order whenever we observe order. But when we look, what we find is complex orders emerging from relatively simple principles. That's also the case in the emergence of complex orders of human cooperation.

Once one understands how well-defined and legally secure rights make possible far more complex forms of order and human cooperation, the idea of rights becomes far more plausible. But how do we protect them? That's where the third leg of the libertarian tripod is needed.

Constitutionally Limited Government

Rights are realized and protected in a wide variety of ways. People who use their own fists to fight back against aggression or their own feet to flee from it are defending their rights to

life, liberty, and estate. We also protect our rights by investing in locks for our doors and keyed ignition systems for our
vehicles, both of which keep potential rights violators out
of what is ours. But a world in which we had to rely only
on our own force to defend ourselves or solely on locks and
keys would most likely be one in which the powerful would
dominate the weak. That's why people form associations,
of infinite variety, for their own defense. In modern free
societies, we rarely resort to immediate violence to defend
ourselves (although it is occasionally necessary); for one
thing, violence generally has subsided as the potential gains
from violence have diminished in comparison to the losses
aggressors are likely to incur from their aggression. Violence
is, for most people, a gradually diminishing feature of their
interaction with each other (except, that is, for the violence of
the state, which sometimes results in hundreds of thousands
or millions of deaths). We rely on specialized agencies to
help us adjudicate disputes (courts and arbitration) and to
defend our rights (security agencies and police). The danger
is that, when we authorize people to use force, even if merely
to defend rights, we may be victimized by those we have
authorized to defend us. The problem is often phrased as in
the words of the Roman poet Juvenal, "Quis custodiet ipsos
custodes?"—who watches the watchmen?

That is one of the most important questions of political
science and has always been emphasized by libertarians, who
have been at the forefront of movements to limit power.
Among the traditional institutions and practices of limiting
power are: constitutions that both establish the powers of
law enforcement and at the same time subject those who
exercise such powers to the law; creation of competing systems of "checks and balances" among different branches of
government; insistence on the right of exit from unjust or
disagreeable political and legal arrangements; written bills
of rights, including the right to freedom of speech, the right
to keep and bear arms, the right to trial by jury, the right

to be secure in the enjoyment of one's property; and other mechanisms that varied by country, culture, and time.

Those traditions may reach back to ancient pacts to limit the powers of kings, such as Magna Carta in England and the Golden Bull of Hungary, or to more recent forms of federalism, as in Switzerland, Australia, the United States, and in post-war Germany and Austria. The latter two implemented federal states as a means to avoid another catastrophe such as the national socialism of the "Third Reich," which plunged Europe into horrific war. Implementation can never be perfect and varies widely according to the history of a country, the strength of various institutions, and other factors, but constitutional restraints on power are the important third pillar of libertarianism.[44]

Liberty, Order, Justice, Peace, and Prosperity

When governments are limited to protecting well-defined individual rights and providing and enforcing the rules of just conduct, individuals will enjoy freedom to order their own affairs and to seek happiness in their own ways, and society will be characterized by greater degrees of complex order and coordination than would have been possible had government sought directly to create such orders by means of coercion. The libertarian tripod is built out of elements—individual rights, spontaneous order, and constitutionally limited government—that have long histories.

A free world is, of course, an imperfect world, for it will be filled with imperfect people, none of whom may be trusted with coercive powers, for even the best will succumb to the temptation to exercise power arbitrarily, to victimize others, to be unjust. That is why constitutional mechanisms are necessary to restrain power.

But libertarianism is not only a vision of constraint. It is also a vision of social, scientific, and artistic progress; of peaceful co-existence and mutual respect among a myriad different ways of life and culture; of industry, commerce, and technology eradicating poverty and pushing back the frontiers of ignorance; of free, independent, and dignified individuals secure in the enjoyment of their rights.

Libertarianism offers both an intellectual project, a way to understand and relate important ideas to each other, and a practical project, the realization of a world of freedom, justice, and peace. For those with the courage to take it up, the project of liberty is inspiring, indeed.

5

"THE TIMES, THEY ARE A-CHANGIN'": LIBERTARIANISM AS ABOLITIONISM

By James Padilioni, Jr.

One of the greatest libertarian causes of all time was the campaign to abolish the greatest violation of liberty: slavery. That spirit informs libertarianism as a political force among young people today. James Padilioni, vice chairman of the North American Executive Board of Students For Liberty and a member of the International Executive Board, is a graduate student in American studies at the College of William and Mary.

"It is my deep, solid, deliberate conviction that this is a cause worth dying for," Angelina Grimke concluded an 1835 letter. The letter was to William Lloyd Garrison, editor of *The Liberator,* the most famous abolitionist publication of its day. The cause was abolition of slavery. She reminded Garrison that "the ground upon which you stand is holy ground: never, never surrender it."[47] The abolitionist movement was no mere social trend. It embodied the conscious decisions of many individuals to step into history and plead with their societies to change their course. Slavery had existed since the beginning of recorded history, and as Orlando Patterson has noted, "There is nothing notably peculiar about the institution of

39

slavery. . . . There is no region on earth that has not at some time harbored the institution. Probably there is no group of people whose ancestors were not at one time slaves or slaveholders."[48] The ubiquity of slavery throughout history gave the institution a certain legitimacy, the legitimacy of familiarity, one that all long-standing traditions—cultural, social, and political alike—tend to develop.

However, after the articulation and promotion of the ideas of individual rights, limited government, and political economy during the Enlightenment, the evolving moral consciousness embedded in those ideas could no longer coexist peacefully with the coercion, lawlessness, and violent control imposed on slaves.[49] That was especially true after the adoption of the Declaration of Independence and its insistence that "all men are created equal." Inspired by their newfound moral awareness, the early libertarians, including the leaders of the abolitionist movements, worked to shape a world in which the institutions of law, politics, and culture would be in harmony with liberty. To the abolitionists, the just cause of freedom weighed more heavily than the enormity of the task that lay before them; in fact, the grim reality of their present served as a catalyst to fuel their activism. Unshakeable in their conviction that "[t]he personal liberty of one man [could] never be the property of another," they launched the greatest human rights campaign in history.[50]

Encouraged by the success of abolitionism, liberals turned next to the unequal status of women, who were, as Mary Wollstonecraft explained, "treated as a kind of subordinate beings, and not as a part of the human species."[51] In 1848, prominent abolitionists Elizabeth Cady Stanton, Lucretia Mott, and Frederick Douglass met in New York at the Seneca Falls Convention to address the issue directly. That meeting resulted in the Declaration of Sentiments. Echoing the phrases of the Declaration of Independence, they proclaimed:

> We hold these truths to be self-evident: that all men and women are created equal; . . . The history of mankind is a history of repeated injuries and usurpations on the part of man toward woman, having in direct object the establishment of an absolute tyranny over her . . . in view of the unjust laws above mentioned, and because women do feel themselves aggrieved, oppressed, and fraudulently deprived of their most sacred rights, we insist that they have immediate admission to all the rights and privileges which belong to them as citizens of these United States.[52]

They were not naïve about the enormous task they faced. Educating society to adopt new values and change old habits would not come easily and their views on historical change reflected this. Frederick Douglass emphasized.

> Let me give you a word of the philosophy of reform. The whole history of the progress of human liberty shows that all concessions yet made to her august claims have been born of earnest struggle. The conflict has been exciting, agitating, all-absorbing, and for the time being, putting all other tumults to silence. It must do this or it does nothing. If there is no struggle there is no progress. Those who profess to favor freedom and yet deprecate agitation are men who want crops without plowing up the ground; they want rain without thunder and lightning. They want the ocean without the awful roar of its many waters. This struggle may be a moral one, or it may be a physical one, and it may be both moral and physical, but it must be a struggle. Power concedes nothing without a demand. It never did and it never will.[53]

Likewise, the reformers at Seneca were fully aware that "[i]n entering upon the great work before us, we anticipate no small amount of misconception, misrepresentation, and ridicule."

Yet they proceeded, undaunted by fear and buoyed by their belief in the justness of their cause, which was the cause of equal freedom for every human being.[54]

Lest anyone believe that the story of the struggle against chattel slavery is uniquely American, it was also fought in other parts of the world. (It is, I am sad to say, still an ongoing struggle in some places.) It was abolished slowly in some places, rapidly in others. The slave trade and then slavery were abolished in the British Empire, thanks to consumer boycotts of slave-produced sugar and the tireless agitation of such figures as William Wilberforce, whose fifty years of work on behalf of freedom are elegantly depicted in the motion picture *Amazing Grace*. Other, less brutal and crushing forms of bondage were also swept away by the tide of libertarian agitation. Serfdom, in particular, disintegrated as an institution in Western Europe, but it was smashed and torn down in Eastern Europe due to the crusading efforts of liberal reformers. The liberation of the Jews from their subordinate status and their entry into full and equal civil rights was also a fruit of liberal agitation.

As the liberal message continued to sweep the world, changing hearts and minds, other longstanding forms of oppression were torn down. Belief in the power of free trade and markets, for instance, spurred the development of Britain's Anti-Corn League in the early nineteenth century, which succeeded in abolishing the tariffs that kept the price of British corn high. By blocking (or taxing at higher rates) foreign imports, those laws benefited politically connected grain growers at the expense of Britain's poor, who then spent the majority of their income on food. The Corn Laws were, as the great Richard Cobden thundered, responsible for the "general distress . . . spread through the country," and in 1849, he and his colleagues, who had pushed for over thirty years for their repeal, witnessed the triumph of free trade over protectionism.[55]

The idea of liberty, whether known as liberalism, classical liberalism, libertarianism, or under other names, has transformed our world. It has been especially successful at enacting such deep and lasting changes because it has depended, not on unanimous, lock-step agreement on means, but rather on the recognition that there are many roads along which one can effect social change.

For example, while some American abolitionists formed the Liberty Party in 1848 (adopting Lysander Spooner's "The Unconstitutionality of Slavery" as their party platform), others chose to work in non-electoral reform movements. They maintained that any "political reformation is to be effected solely by a change in the moral vision of the people;—not by attempting to prove, that it is the duty of every abolitionist to be a voter, but that it is the duty of every voter to be an abolitionist."[56] And despite the fact that leading abolitionists such as Wendell Phillips scoffed, "We do not *play* politics," the abolitionists ultimately succeeded both morally *and* politically.[57] As intellectual historian Louis Menand observed, "The abolitionists were not apolitical. The renunciation of politics was the secret of their politics."[58]

Institutional and political change are daunting, but they are necessary for the experience of freedom. Unjust laws must be repealed and oppression undone for human beings to be free. Those changes are both cause and effect of changes in the minds of human beings; changes in how they think, but also changes in how they decide to act. Libertarians may focus on changing ideas, or on changing laws, or on changing institutions, or on changing other elements of society. There is no unique way to advance liberty; there are as many ways as there are human capabilities, interests, and passions. Changing perceptions can have an enormous impact on institutions. The changing perception of the slave—"Am I not a man and a brother?" was the motto on the great entrepreneur Josiah Wedgwood's famous cameo that promoted the abolitionist cause—had its impact. The changing perception of gay people in the US in recent years has helped to drive huge changes, first in the private sector, where firms introduced policies to attract and retain gay employees, and then in the political sector, as states decriminalized same-sex relationships (it's hard to imagine that people were imprisoned for years for loving another person), the US Supreme Court declared "sodomy laws" an unconstitutional infringement on liberty, and states began to establish equal rights for gay people to marry.

To return to the definitive cause of abolition of slavery, it is wise to remember that the abolitionists did not embrace their cause for the sake of being contrarian. They knew that the struggle would be long and it would be difficult, and they soberly employed moral suasion, social education, political agitation, and many other techniques to do away with slavery, then with the subjugation of women. Many of those reformers started when they were young and did not allow their vision of a free and just future to be dimmed by conformism, by "practicality," by false appeals to a pseudo-realism that insisted that one get along by going along, that one give up dreams of justice and liberty for the practical business of getting a job, a good post at university, a position in government or the church, at the small cost of averting one's eyes from injustice. Those who undertook the task of eliminating slavery had their eyes opened. They saw what was about them. And they refused to accept it. We are the beneficiaries of their vision.

The philosophy of liberty is fueled by the knowledge that the injustices of today need not continue into the future. Cultures can change. Ideas can change. Politics and institutions can change. That is what unites the classical liberals of yesteryear to the young libertarians of today. It is the energy of youth coupled with the intellectual grasp of the promise and the imperative of individual human freedom, spurred on by a passion to see injustice vanquished. It is a potent combination, indeed. The young libertarians of today travel a path that has been blazed by the libertarians of the past. We have inherited much, but the work is far from over. Every law today that erects barriers to voluntary transactions and limits unhindered freedom of thought and expression ought to be abolished and every act of plunder, coercion, and violence ought to be resisted. It has fallen to our generation to follow that path, as our forebears did before us. The status quo cannot, and will not, be the status quo forever; that is the nature of change. The future ahead of us is the future we choose to create. A previous generation mobilized to oppose war and to oppose the evils of racial segregation, movements given voice by Bob Dylan's moving lyrics: "Your old road is rapidly agin' / Please get out of the new one / If you can't lend your hand / For the times they are a-changin'."[59]

It was with such determination that the twenty-five-year-old William Lloyd Garrison boldly launched his publication *The Liberator:*

> I will be as harsh as truth, and as uncompromising as justice. On this subject, I do not wish to think, or to speak, or write, with moderation. No! No! Tell a man whose house is on fire to give a moderate alarm; tell him to moderately rescue his wife from the hands of the ravisher; tell the mother to gradually extricate her babe from the fire into which it has fallen;—but urge me not to use moderation in a cause like the present. I am in earnest—I will not equivocate—I will not excuse—I will not retreat a single inch—AND I WILL BE HEARD.[60]

We, the Students For Liberty, are abolitionists. And we will be heard.

6

THE POLITICAL
PRINCIPLE OF LIBERTY

By Alexander McCobin

A political theory or ideology has three components: justification, principle, and policy. Libertarianism is situated at the level of principle, which allows libertarians to draw from a wide variety of philosophical traditions, religions, and ways of life. Alexander McCobin, president and co-founder of Students For Liberty and a PhD student in philosophy at Georgetown University, shows how and why libertarianism has universal appeal.

What is libertarianism? And what is it not? Is it an encompassing philosophical system that tells us the meaning of existence, of truth, of art, and of life? Is it a moral philosophy that tells us how to lead better lives? Or is it a political philosophy that makes possible the coexistence of many peaceful philosophies of life and morality, a framework for voluntary social interaction? Both those who embrace libertarianism and those who don't would benefit from some clarity about what the term means.

To cut to the chase, libertarianism is a political philosophy that prioritizes the principle of liberty.

In plain language, you can be a libertarian and be a Hindu, a Christian, a Jew, a Muslim, a Buddhist, a Deist, an agnostic, an atheist, or a follower of any other religion, so long as you respect the equal rights of others. You can like hip hop, Rachmaninoff's concertos, reggae, Brahms, Chinese opera, or any other kind of music or none at all. One could go on with examples, but those should suffice. Libertarianism is not a philosophy of life or love or metaphysics or religion or art or value, although it's certainly compatible with an infinite variety of such philosophies.

So what is a political philosophy? A political philosophy has three components: justification, principle, and policy. The justification for a political philosophy is the standard used to justify one's beliefs; that could mean achieving the greatest good for the greatest number, respect for the autonomy of our fellow humans as moral beings, fairness in the distribution of burdens and benefits, or something else. Principles are the abstract statements that specify how those justified beliefs are realized. Policy is the practical application of those principles to specific, real-world problems. In daily political life, policy is at the center of discussion and concern, dealing with questions such as, "Should we raise (or lower) taxes?" "Should we go to war with another country?" and "Should smoking marijuana be forbidden?"

The principles that underlie one's policy positions sometimes come out when people ask, "Should we care more about following the Constitution or helping those in need?" Questions like that sometimes reveal the principles people prioritize and on which they ground their views on policies. The justification of those principles is usually reserved for philosophical conversations, when people ask questions such as, "Should liberty be preferred over equality?" and "By what standard would we decide between the Constitution and the needs of the indigent?"

Libertarianism is not a comprehensive political philosophy that offers definitive guidance in all matters, from justification to policy prescriptions. Libertarianism is defined by a commitment to a mid-level principle of liberty. That principle may be justified by various persons in various ways. (In fact, the principle of liberty may be—and often is—justified as a principle by multiple standards; it may be justified on the basis of respect for autonomy *and* on the basis of generating widespread prosperity. There's no need to choose which is the "true justification" if both converge on the same principle.) Moreover, the application of the principle of liberty to policy issues may lead to debate and disagreement, depending on one's evaluation of the circumstances, of the facts of a case, and so on.

It should be emphasized that a commitment to the political principle of liberty does not require any libertarian to endorse what people do with their liberty. One might condemn someone for disgraceful, immoral, rude, or unconscionable conduct while defending the right of that person to behave that way, again, so long as the behavior did not violate the rights of others.

The Political Principle of Liberty

Libertarianism's commitments are limited to the level of principles. Specifically, libertarianism is committed to the principle of the presumption of liberty: all persons should be free to do what they wish with their lives and their rights, unless there is a sufficient reason (the violation of the equal rights of others) to restrain them. Every human being has the right to liberty. Holders of other political philosophies ground their policy prescriptions on other principles, such as:

- Fraternity – The principle that people should be responsible for the lives of others.
- Equality of Outcomes – The principle that people should end up in similar positions, with similar goods, levels of utility, or some other desirable outcome.[45]

One might ask: Is there a better way to articulate the principle of liberty? Perhaps. The Cato Institute's motto is "individual liberty, limited government, free markets, and peace." Is that the best way to spell out the liberty principle, or is it misleading to segment that principle into different areas, since, for example, "free markets" and "peace" could be seen as merely different facets of the principle of liberty? The best or most useful formulation may depend on circumstances, and as the Cato Institute is mainly a public policy research institute, their formulation seems to work well for them.

Justifications for Liberty

A philosophy that argues for one principle or set of principles and rejects others needs a justification for why the one is chosen and others are not. The choice among principles requires justification. Some might argue that "each person owns himself or herself and may thus make all decisions regarding his or her own body and property," but even that would require, not merely further articulation (e.g., what is "ownership" and what acts does "regarding" cover), but would itself stand in need of some deeper level of justification. Without a justification, it's just a claim. There is a great diversity of justifications for the principle of liberty. Over the years many have been advanced, defended, debated, and criticized by libertarians and continue to be debated today. Here are a few, followed in each case by a thinker who justifies liberty at least primarily on that ground:

- Utility – Liberty ought to be the principle of political life because it creates the greatest good for the greatest number of people (Jeremy Bentham);
- Autonomy – Limited government and respect for equal rights are the appropriate framework for respecting the autonomy of moral agents (Robert Nozick);
- The Rational Pursuit of One's Own Life and Happiness – Liberty is a requirement of pursuing happiness in accordance with human nature (Ayn Rand);
- Natural Law and Natural Rights – Liberty is a feature of man's nature as a being that is both self-directing and social (John Locke);

- Revelation – Liberty is a grant from God, and accordingly no one has the right to take it upon himself or herself to take from another that with which we are endowed by God (John Locke and Thomas Jefferson);
- Sympathy – Liberty emerges as the "simple system" that accords with the human ability to put oneself in the place of another (Adam Smith);
- Agreement – The principle of liberty is justified as the necessary result of mutual agreement among rational agents (Jan Narveson);
- Humility – Liberty is justified as a principle of political organization because no one can know what would be needed to direct the lives of others (F. A. Hayek);
- Fairness – Liberty is justified because it is the most effective means to benefit the least well-off in society (John Tomasi).

Note that that is not a comprehensive list. Moreover, one could rely on more than one justification for a political principle. The key point is that, although libertarianism need not rely exclusively upon any particular justification, it does not stand without justification. Libertarianism as such is not committed to any particular justification for the principle of liberty.

The principle of liberty provides guidance for human conduct, but it is not a self-justifying principle. While libertarianism is not a comprehensive political philosophy, individuals may embrace libertarianism because of their commitment to deeper justificatory values, such as human flourishing, autonomy, reason, happiness, religious precepts, sympathy, or fairness.

One Principle, Variant Policies

Similarly, just as there may be multiple justifications for a principle, there may be variations among libertarians as to how to apply the liberty principle. There are open debates on many topics, including patents and copyrights (a property right based on creativity or a government grant of monopoly?), the death penalty for convicted murderers (a just retribution or a dangerous power?), abortion (a contentious issue depending on whether one believes that there are two agents with moral rights involved, or just one), taxation (is it just theft, or are some taxes to pay for authentically collective goods, such as defense, legitimate charges for services?), foreign and military policy (all libertarians agree that there is a presumption against war, but there is disagreement about what would be sufficient to rebut that presumption and justify military force), and even gay marriage (should the state stop discriminating against gay couples, or should the state simply get out of the business of marriage altogether, leaving it to contract law?). Reasonable people can certainly differ on how to apply a principle.

That doesn't mean that there are no libertarian policies. Laws against murder, rape, slavery, and theft are fundamental to any civilized legal system; they should even be applied to governments. Nonetheless, it's often not obvious what specific policies are required to enforce such general laws. Here again, reasonable people may differ. The appropriate steps that governments or citizens may take to protect citizens and their families from violence, for example, are subject to debate.

Halfway measures are also matter for debate. For example: should libertarians endorse the decriminalization of marijuana use for medicinal purposes, even though a consistent application of the liberty principle would decriminalize marijuana without constraints on its purpose? Is it a "sell out" of principle or a step toward greater freedom? Reasonable people may differ.

The Difference Between Politics and Ethics

Libertarianism is a political philosophy, not an ethical philosophy. Ethics is concerned with the right or the good because it is the right or the good. It seeks to identify that which is right or good on its own. While related, political philosophy is concerned with a different area of human conduct. Political philosophy is concerned with the right kinds of relationships people may have with one another. There is often significant overlap between those philosophical areas because they both prescribe codes of conduct for human beings and address how people ought to act both when on their own and when interacting with others. However, they are separated according to the justification they offer for why an individual ought to follow the code of conduct.

Ethical actions are justified on the grounds that the agent is doing something because she is a moral being. Her moral agency guides her conduct to act rightly. Ethics begins with the individual moral agent and asks, "How ought an individual act *because she is a moral agent*?" The code of conduct in a political philosophy, however, is justified on the grounds that the agent must respect other individuals as separate moral agents. It is a social philosophy that seeks to articulate how people ought to treat one another from the perspective of interacting with others. It asks the question: "How ought an individual act *because she is interacting with other individuals*?"

In other words: the origin of morality is the self: how people ought to act because they, themselves are human beings. The origin of political philosophy is others: the requirement to treat others justly because other people are human beings.

That does not mean that ethical consideration excludes the concerns of others in codes of conduct. To determine what an ethical action would be in many situations, we must consider how our action affects others or adopt another person's ends and concerns as our own. However, the focus of this concern is still on the actor's moral agency. The way we care about individuals in an ethical manner is to consider them as part of our own moral agency. In contrast, the way we care about individuals in accordance with political philosophy is to consider them as separate moral agents that deserve respect, and thus require limits on our agency in a manner that respects them.

Since most human activity involves interactions with others, both ethical and political rules may be applied to the same situations, which sometimes leads people to conflate political philosophy and ethics. Some people attempt to legislate morality, because they believe that if something is immoral, it obviously ought to be illegal. If people ought not do it, then others should prevent them from doing it. A common response to this is to say that "people have different moralities" and they ought not impose "their morality" on others. One need not, however, embrace moral relativism ("my morality" is as good or valid as "your morality") to embrace liberty. Indeed, such relativism would be a very weak foundation for liberty, for if all such claims are as good as all others, then why would liberty be any better than coercion?

A variant of that argument is that, while there might be a universal morality that applies to everyone, no one knows what it is, so out of our ignorance of the correct morality, we ought not legislate any morality. While a stronger argument than the moral relativist one before, this argument still accepts the idea that "legislating morality" would be legitimate if we could simply determine what the correct morality is. Even when we accept that there is a single, universal morality, and assume that it is widely known and agreed to, legislating morality through political institutions would still be illegitimate because morality deals with a different part of the human experience than does political philosophy. *Morality helps us—we hope—to lead better lives. Law helps us to live justly with each other.*

Some argue that a political philosophy not grounded in a particular ethics has no justification. But recall that the principle that informs a political philosophy is a mid-level claim. It still has a justification (or, perhaps, multiple justifications), but not one that is bootstrapped into the principles of libertarianism. As pointed out above, people with different justifications can still agree on the common principle. In this case, toleration of such diversity is an application of the principle of liberty, which allows a variety of ethical views and behavior, so long as the same rights are enjoyed equally by all. For most situations, morality and political philosophy may indeed prescribe the same conduct: murdering, raping, and stealing are certainly immoral and they are properly punished by law. But there are also cases where morality may require or forbid an act about which political philosophy is silent. It may be that morality requires you to love your neighbor as your brother (or sister), but political philosophy—at least, libertarian political philosophy—does not require that. As even the venerable St. Thomas Aquinas argued, "human law is framed for a number of human beings, the majority of whom are not perfect in virtue. Wherefore human laws do not forbid all vices, from which the virtuous abstain, but only the more grievous vices, from which it is possible for the majority to abstain; and chiefly those that are to the hurt of others, without the prohibition of which human society could not be maintained; thus human law prohibits murder, theft and suchlike."[40] There are many things people find objectionable, immoral, even vicious from the perspective of ethics, but from the perspective of political philosophy they fall into the class of the permissible. The question by which we delineate whether something is legitimately prohibited by law is: would this action violate the rights of another?

Conclusion

Libertarians include people of all religious faith and of none, holders of many different encompassing philosophies, followers of a variety of lifestyles, members of many varied ethnic and linguistic groups, but all are united by a common principle of liberty. They may diverge on particular applications of principle, disagree on relevant facts, and even as a consequence sometimes find themselves on opposite sides of a particular issue, although they subscribe to the same principle of liberty. That principle unites them when they campaign to eliminate victimless crime laws, oppose tyranny, defend freedom of trade and enterprise, oppose aggressive violence, and generally support equal liberty for all.

I invite those in agreement with the political principle of liberty to explore libertarian ideas more seriously, to read about them, to think about them, to discuss them, debate them, compare them with other political philosophies, in short, to use your minds. To support the principle of liberty is to be a libertarian. One person's reason for supporting that principle may be different from the reasons of other libertarians; that's one of the ways that libertarianism differs from most other political philosophies, because it doesn't require unanimity on foundations, just agreement that each person has an equal right to liberty. One libertarian may disagree with another on the most appropriate policy prescriptions to instantiate in the world their commonly held principle. It is the political principle of liberty that defines the philosophy of libertarianism and ties libertarians together. That's all, but it's enough.

7

No Liberty, No Art:
No Art, No Liberty

By Sarah Skwire

Freedom is important for art, as is frequently maintained, but art is also important for freedom. Art disrupts old patterns and makes us think. Art is impossible without freedom, but freedom is impossible without art. Sarah Skwire is a Fellow at the Liberty Fund and is the author of the popular college writing textbook Writing with a Thesis. *She earned her PhD in English at the University of Chicago.*

In 380 BCE, Plato argued that poets were too dangerous to be permitted to live in his ideal republic.

In 8 CE, Ovid was exiled from Rome for what he said was "a poem and an error."

In 722 CE, the Japanese poet Asomioyu Hozumi was exiled to Sado Island for criticizing the emperor.

In 1642 CE, Oliver Cromwell's government ordered the closure of all theaters in London.

In 1815 CE, Goya was brought before the Inquisition, which demanded to know who had commissioned his painting, "The Naked Maja." Shortly afterwards, he lost his position as the Spanish court painter.

In 2012 CE, the Russian punk band Pussy Riot was arrested and sentenced to two years in a penal colony for performing an anti-government song in a cathedral.

To be an artist has always meant to be terrifyingly vulnerable to the controlling hand of the state. Stalin's "Great Purge" of the 1920s and '30s imprisoned two thousand writers, artists, and intellectuals. Approximately fifteen hundred of them died in prison. Hitler's National Socialist government turned control of all the arts over to the Propaganda Ministry in 1933, and the Theresienstadt concentration camp was created specifically to imprison and kill artists and intellectuals. And we still don't know how many artists died, disappeared, or had their lives and their works destroyed forever during the "lost decade" (1966–1976) of Mao's Cultural Revolution.

Those of us who have the pleasure of creating art in the freedom of the twenty-first century West, have the good fortune of not having to think too much about artistic liberty. When we do consider it, however, we often think of it as an aesthetic issue—a personal creative freedom to choose the tools we want and to use the style that speaks to us most deeply. We think of artistic freedom as the fulfillment of our desires to make the images we want and use the words we want without being held to restrictive stylistic guidelines. (As the painter and photographer Ben Shahn once noted, left to choose their own labels, artists would "choose none.") We may be vaguely aware that in 2001, a radio station was fined $7,000 by the FCC for playing Sarah Jones's "Your Revolution Will Not Happen Between These Thighs." And we might laugh at the irony that a rap written to protest the sexual objectification of women in hip hop was characterized as containing "unmistakable patently offensive sexual references" that "appear to be designed to pander and shock."

We tend to dismiss these seemingly minor examples of suppression. In twenty-first century Western culture, artistic censorship is for the small-minded, the easily shocked. It's for the fools who protest Harry Potter on the grounds that it encourages Satanism, or for those who create the Parental Music Resource Center's list of the "Filthy Fifteen" rock songs that are too dangerous for kids to hear. As the playwright

Eugene O'Neill said, "Censorship of anything, at any time, in any place, on whatever pretense, has always been and always will be the last resort of the boob and the bigot."

And we know it, so we laugh. But maybe we shouldn't. Small fines and warning labels are easy to learn to live with, but they also may encourage artists to limit their subject matter and second guess the fullest expression of their creativity. And that's an easy first step to some very bad things.

We should not forget, simply because we do have great artistic freedom, that the liberty to create is a fragile liberty. We should not forget how vulnerable we are. And we should not forget how often throughout history, artistic liberty has been destroyed.

Forgetting all of that would be a tragedy, and not just because it means we lose our memory of the sacrifices made for art and liberty by those who came before us. It would be a tragedy because it means losing sight of the power art has to work for liberty.

I want to be clear here that when I speak about the power of art to work for liberty, I do not only mean didactic art—those forms of expression that explicitly promote liberty or question state power. Certainly that kind of art can be enormously affective and effective. The contemporary street art produced by artists such as Banksy and the music of folk singer Frank Turner are fine examples of the enormous impact that kind of art, done well, can have.

But even art that is not created with the intention of promoting liberty is art that works for liberty. The arrest and trial of the Czech rock band "The Plastic People of the Universe" spurred the Velvet Revolution not because their music was overtly political, but because, as Václav Havel wrote, "The freedom to play rock music was understood as a human freedom and thus as essentially the same as the freedom to engage in philosophical and political reflection, the freedom to write, the freedom to express and defend the various social and political interests of society." Living "within the truth" turns out to be impossible if a society and its members are not free to make art.

Monty Python member Eric Idle helps to explain why that is the case. "At least one way of measuring the freedom of any society is the amount of comedy that is permitted, and clearly a healthy society permits more satirical comment than a repressive," he wrote. While it is possible to find overt political meaning in some of Monty Python's work—*Life of Brian* and *Monty Python and the Holy Grail* in particular—Idle's argument suggests that the mere creation of comedy is a political act, an act that by its very nature works for liberty. The Parrot Sketch is, simply by existing, as much of a blow for liberty as the debate over the legitimacy of different forms of government in *Holy Grail*. "Irreverence" said Mark Twain, "is the champion of liberty and its one sure defense."

Art can be disruptive. In whatever form it takes, it forces the observer to readjust old ideas, reconsider old perceptions, and reformat old programming. Emily Dickinson said, "If I feel physically as if the whole top of my head were taken off, I know that is poetry." e. e. cummings described the same feeling when he wrote that his idea of poetic technique could be expressed "in fifteen words, by quoting The Eternal Question And Immortal Answer of burlesk, viz., 'Would you hit a woman with a child?—No, I'd hit her with a brick.'" And Margaret Atwood creates that experience on the page for her reader in the poem, "You Fit Into Me":

> You fit into me
> like a hook into an eye
>
> a fish hook
> an open eye

Art happens in the moment when our perceptions shift: the Pointilist painting seen from one foot away and again from across the room; the contrast between Laurence Olivier's and Kenneth Branagh's films of Shakespeare's *Henry V*; Pop Art's insistence on treating the everyday object as a work of art; John Cage's assertion that silence is its own music. Art requires that we consistently readjust our expectations and re-examine what we think we know. The experience of art, as creator or as audience, trains us in flexible thinking. That is, in itself, a kind of freedom.

But it is not just the sense of freedom that accompanies our aesthetic response that makes me say art advances for liberty. Art demands that we think. But it does not demand that we think only one thing. It gives us the liberty to express the multiplicity of our opinions. Art, like liberty, has no patience for ideology. Walt Whitman wrote:

> Do I contradict myself?
> Very well then I contradict myself,
> (I am large, I contain multitudes.)

Ralph Waldo Emerson similarly observed that "a foolish consistency is the hobgoblin of little minds, adored by little statesmen and philosophers and divines. With consistency a great soul has simply nothing to do." For many artists, the notion of having a fixed and final opinion on a subject simply does not make sense. Understanding emerges through the process of creating art—as knowledge emerges through the interactions of a free society, or prices emerge through the interactions of a free market. Graham Wallas, cofounder of the London School of Economics, once wrote, "The little girl had the making of a poet in her who, being told to be sure of her meaning before she spoke, said, 'How can I know what I think till I see what I say?'" Art allows us to decide that we think *odi et amo* both at once—I hate and I love. It gives us the chance to celebrate the heroism of Henry V while mourning the costs of war. And it reveals that more than one thing can be true at a time, that there can be multiple perspectives on the same scene.

Art allows for ideas to play creatively. It is from precisely this sort of creative play that the greatest innovations arise. That is what scientist Matt Ridley means when he says that "[y]ou need to understand how human beings bring together their brains and enable their ideas to combine and recombine, to meet and, indeed, to mate. In other words, you need to understand how ideas have sex." This is the kind of artistic and intellectual free space praised by Ronald Reagan—who was an actor long before he was a politician—when he said that "[i]n an atmosphere of liberty, artists and patrons are free to think the unthinkable and create the audacious; they are free to make both horrendous mistakes and glorious celebrations."

Such audacious creations—such fertile mating of minds—happen everywhere, even under the worst of conditions. Art, after all, is produced in the most oppressive regimes and in the darkest prisons. Musician and libertarian Lindy Vopnfjord says, "The desire for liberty is the most powerful force for creativity in an artist; that is why even in the most oppressive places some of the most beautiful and powerful art is made." Shockingly, some have suggested that the persistent vitality of the artistic spirit in the face of oppression suggests that, for the best art, you need a little tyranny. Federico Fellini argues that "[l]eft on his own, free to do anything he likes, the artist ends up doing nothing at all. If there's one thing that's dangerous for an artist, it's precisely this question of total freedom, waiting for inspiration and all the rest of it." If the artist has nothing against which to protest, what will spur the creative impulse?

That's one view. But Albert Camus insists that any restraint must be self-generated. He writes, "Without freedom, no art; art lives only on the restraints it imposes on itself, and dies of all others." A rule taken on willingly as an artistic challenge differs fundamentally from an externally imposed diktat. Keats makes the same argument in his poem "On the Sonnet" when he writes: ". . . if we must be constrain'd, / . . . if we may not let the Muse be free, / She will be bound with garlands of her own." And so we must preserve our art and protect it from those who would impose their unacceptable constraints on our audacious creations—whether they claim to do so "for our own good" or "for the good of society."

Ivan Grigoryevich, the central character in Russian writer Vasily Grossman's novel *Forever Flowing*, argued that it is futile to think of our artistic, social, and political freedoms as separable.

> I used to think freedom was freedom of speech, freedom of the press, freedom of conscience. But freedom is the whole life of everyone. Here is what it amounts to: You have to have the right to sow what you wish to, to make shoes or coats, to bake into bread the flour ground from the grain you have sown, and to sell it or not sell it as you wish; for the lathe operator, the steelworker, and the artist it's a matter of being able to live as you wish and work as you wish and not as they order you to. And in our country there is no freedom—not for those who write books nor for those who sow grain nor for those who make shoes.

Artists have died for their use of the cameras, the brushes, the pens, the chisels, the instruments, the dancing shoes we use to make our art. It is up to us, then, to use those same tools to make our art as we like and to do our work as we like, and to make possible the art and the liberty of others. Art is born from liberty, and it gives birth to liberty in turn. It is trivial and vital, grotesque and beautiful. It will not, on its own, save us. But without it, we cannot be saved. Art, as Richard Wilbur said, "is always a matter, my darling, / Of life or death, as I had forgotten."

8

THE HUMBLE CASE
FOR LIBERTY

By Aaron Ross Powell

Libertarianism is a philosophy with radical implications. Those implications are drawn, not from a claim to know what's best for others, but from a strong dose of skepticism about one's own knowledge, which means about one's ability to run the lives of other people. Humility, a virtue and the result of a skeptical attitude, is both an ingredient in a good life and a foundation for liberty. Aaron Ross Powell is a Research Fellow at the Cato Institute and editor of the institute's Libertarianism.org *project, which is developing the largest web portal of libertarian scholarship and material. He earned his JD at the University of Denver.*

I could be wrong about pretty much anything. What I don't know so outweighs what I do that my actual knowledge appears as little more than a small raft on an ocean of ignorance.

I suffer no shame admitting this unflattering fact, not only because there's never any shame in acknowledging the truth, but also because everyone else is in the same boat. Our ignorance—what we don't know—always and enormously outweighs our knowledge. It's true of even the smartest and most educated.

Recognizing that fact ought to humble us. And that humility, informed by a realistic picture of how government operates, ought to make us libertarians. Libertarianism is a philosophy of humility. It's one that takes us as we are and grants us the freedom to make as much of ourselves as we can. And it's a philosophy that understands just how damaging human failings can be when coupled with the coercive force of government. Libertarianism limits rulers because it recognizes that rulers are just ordinary people who exercise extraordinary power—and that the harm that power can inflict more often than not outweighs any good it might achieve. Libertarianism rests on humility and refuses to tolerate the hubris of those who would consider themselves higher and mightier than others.

Let's start by looking at what it means to have a humble view of our claims to knowledge. Each of us certainly seems to know quite a lot, from what we ate this morning to the number of moons circling Mars. We know that George Washington was the first president of the United States of America, that Boris Yeltsin was the first president of the Russian Federation, and that driving while drunk is a bad idea.

But if we look to the whole of intellectual history, we see one overturned conviction after another. What was scientific truth three hundred years ago is balderdash today. Our brightest once believed that you could understand a person's mind and character by studying the bumps on his or her head. (It was given the scientific sounding name of "phrenology.") The wise and the great were once certain that the Earth sat at the center of the universe.

It's not just science that can't seem to finally and forever get it right. Very smart people have argued about deep philosophical problems for as long as there have been very smart people. Two and a half millennia ago, Plato thought he'd figured out what justice is. Most philosophers since have disagreed—but none have offered an alternative that wasn't itself open to strong counter-argument.

We ought to always be skeptical of claims to absolute knowledge. If you believe a philosophical point is settled, you're almost certainly wrong. If you believe science today understands a topic fully, you're likely to find in just a few years that it didn't. Furthermore, if we're properly skeptical about humanity's knowledge in general, we ought to be even more skeptical about proclamations of certainty from individual members of our species.

But all of that doesn't stop many of us from often feeling like there's just no way we could be wrong.

It was in college that I first began to understand how common such intellectual hubris is. I was baffled by how broadly many of my professors saw their own expertise. A PhD in early twentieth-century American comedic film felt qualified to critique the cutting edge of physics research and to lecture his students on which types of cancer ought to get the most funding. It happens outside the university, too, especially in politics. How many Americans look at the fantastic complexity of our health care delivery system and say, "Oh, I know how to fix that"? How many voters without even basic knowledge of economics think it's clear which candidate's proposals will promote prosperity? It takes some effort to admit that we could be wrong about the things we think we have good reason to believe. But at the very least, it ought to be easier to recognize when we clearly know nothing about a topic.

Furthermore, many of us aren't adequately skeptical about the move from knowledge of facts to knowledge of values. Take nutritionists, for example. They believe they know which foods are most healthy, that is, which give us the most nutrients with the least harmful other stuff. If we consume substance X, we can expect result Y. (Of course, even that knowledge has changed dramatically in recent years.) But notice this "is" doesn't get us to an "ought." What's healthy is a different question entirely from what I ought to eat.

I can recognize that fried potatoes aren't as healthy as steamed broccoli while still being right that I ought to eat French fries for dinner tonight. That's because what I ought to eat doesn't necessarily mean the same thing as what's healthiest for me. "Ought" can include other values, too, such as the pleasure I'll get, the varying prices of the alternatives, and so on. Nutrition speaks to the one value (what's healthy), but it has nothing to say about the rest.

Proper skepticism applies to both others and to us. I should be skeptical about your claims of absolute certainty, and I should likewise be skeptical about the veracity of my own.

Such skepticism shouldn't make us abandon all claims to knowledge, of course. But it should lead us to adopt an attitude of humility. Knowing others face the same difficulties in ascertaining truth, we should expect humility from them, as well.

This is where humility urges us in the direction of libertarianism. If we embrace legitimate skepticism about our knowledge of both truth and values, then we should hesitate before compelling people who may disagree with us to live by our convictions. We should hesitate, in other words, before reaching for a club or calling on the police to use their nightsticks.

Why? Any policy may turn out to be bad or ineffective, but can't we always go back and fix it? And what of the gains to be had in trying to make the world better by coercing others, either by our own force, or via state action, even if it means occasionally making things worse for some people? If we're pretty sure our values are correct and our facts support them, then what's the harm in using politics to make everyone else comply?

To show what's wrong with that line of thinking, it may help to think about the purpose of life. The ancient Greek philosopher Aristotle believed the only thing desired for its own sake is the achievement of eudaimonia—usually translated as "happiness" or "flourishing."

Aristotle believed that eudaimonia isn't something found in discrete moments of pleasure or pain (what we often mean when we say, "I'm happy") but instead is found only in an assessment of a life taken as a whole. At the end of a life, we look back and ask, "Was it good?" Everything we are, every reason we have for being, is bound up in being able to answer "yes" when our time comes.

Aristotle had his own idea of the best life, the life that exhibited eudaimonia to the highest degree. He thought it meant living in accord with that which is uniquely human: our capacity to reason. Thus the highest and best life was one spent in contemplation. Perhaps it is not surprising that one of the world's greatest philosophers thought happiness flowed from a life of philosophy.

For Aristotle, of course, it did. But just as we need to recognize the limits of our knowledge about the external world, we must also be humble in our prescriptions of the recipe for the good life. Happiness for me may not be the same thing as happiness for you. There is no generic "human being" who is happy, but billions of very diverse human beings. Happiness may be found in reason, but it can also come through raising children, experiencing great art, building a successful business, becoming an athlete, or helping those less fortunate. And if the good life for each individual is bound up in the specific features of their lives, so too are the paths to achieving it. How I go about making my life good can vary from the way you do—not just in the goals we each aim at but also in the ways we assure our aim is true.

While Aristotle may have gotten some of the details wrong, I think he was right about the broad picture. Most people want to live good, satisfying lives—and a good life is, we might say, a life lived in pursuit of the good life. As the American founders put it in the Declaration of Independence, it's "the pursuit of happiness." Our various pursuits may take different paths, depending on our circumstances, interests, and values. It's the pursuit that matters.

Respecting each other—recognizing each other's dignity as self-directing (what the philosophers call "autonomous") beings—means respecting different forms of that quest. It means not actively inhibiting each other in our pursuits of the good—and recognizing the right each of us has to choose his or her own path.

I've come to the conclusion that that necessarily entails a state that is radically limited, certainly compared to the actual states we see around the world. To understand why, we need to have a realistic view of how governments operate.

In their private lives, people often act poorly, or pursue their own selfish interests, even when it means harming others. Sometimes they hurt other people just for the thrill of it. Pickpockets steal from strangers, scam artists prey on the elderly. Many people, when they think about government, assume that those undesirable traits vanish when someone enters public office. Politicians abandon selfishness and become motivated only by a desire to promote the public good.

That's silly, of course. People remain themselves, even when given fancy titles and power over the lives of others. Being a politician or a bureaucrat doesn't automatically make one better informed—or better—than the rest of us. There is a group of thinkers who take the realistic approach to understanding government, that people don't change their natures when they enter government; they just change the institutional constraints they face, because they have powers that the rest of us lack. Their school of thought is known as "public choice."

Public choice teaches us that politicians and state officials use the knowledge they have available to make the best decisions they can, with "best" being a product of their own judgment and, of course, also of their own interests. Those interests could, of course, include money and fame, but more often mean simply staying in power.

The result is that politics often means helping the most vocal—the people most visible to politicians—and doing so at the expense of everyone else. That's why the state enacts and maintains such truly awful policies—such as agricultural subsidies that raise food prices and lead to wasteful misuse of resources—that fly in the face of evidence and reason. Few politicians actively want bad policies. Instead, they're motivated by the people who show up: the farmers benefiting from these programs. And, because they can't see as directly the harmful effects their laws and regulations have on everyone else (higher prices of food, reduced variety, etc.), they continue to support policies most of us would be better off without.

Moreover, even those harmed frequently remain unaware of the harm being done. It would cost too much to become informed—more than we could recoup even if we were able to repeal those bad policies. So we remain, as public choice economists say, "rationally ignorant," and since we remain ignorant of the burdens those policies place on us, we aren't able to inform the politicians whom we vote into office. The special interests tend to be "squeakier wheels" than the rest of us.

It's important to recognize that this isn't the result of having "the wrong people" in office. It's not something that can be fixed by electing better leaders. Instead, it's just the way government works when it grows beyond certain narrow limits.

Another fact about government that ought to trouble the humble is just how far its reach extends. Imagine I have very particular values when it comes to educating children, and that I have certain beliefs about the best way to achieve those values. If I don't control the state, my reach extends no further than my kids—and any children whose parents voluntarily participate in my program.

But if I can flex the state's muscle in support of my values and beliefs, I can extend my reach to all the children in my town, or in my state, or even in my entire country. Nobody will have any choice but to bring their children up with the educational values I prefer.

If we're good skeptics, this should concern us deeply, because those beliefs about the best way to educate children may turn out to be incorrect, in which case it's not just a handful of kids harmed, but all of them. And what if parents disagree—as they do—on what "best" even means in this case?

What if they simply have different values when it comes to education? A state without the proper limits forces us into a one-size-fits-all approach—one that assumes some person or group can definitively know what's good for everyone. We should all be skeptical of such claims. We should all take a good dose of humility.

So what are those limits to government? What would a state based on a proper level of skepticism look like? It would be one restricted to providing an environment in which its citizens are free to pursue the good life as each understands it.

We can't meaningfully pursue the good under constant threat of violence, so the state should protect us from others who would do us bodily harm. And we can't acquire and make full use of the resources we need to lead good lives if we aren't secure in our holdings, so the state should act to limit theft—and require thieves to compensate us for those thefts that do occur.

When the state does those things—when it protects us from violence, fraud, and theft—then it fulfills the role of freeing each citizen to pursue the good life in ways as personal and unique as his or her own values.

When the state does more, however—when it takes resources from us beyond what it needs to meet those duties and when it flexes its coercive might to force some of us to live by the values of others—it fails to grant us the dignity we deserve as rational, autonomous human beings. It substitutes its judgments for our own and places barriers in our pursuit of the good life.

In the end, if we need a state, we need it because of its usefulness to us in our pursuits of happiness. We need it for that, and no more. Having the proper degree of humility means recognizing that, no matter how certain we may feel that we have things figured out, we cannot use the state to force others into whichever mold we might prefer. To do so is to succumb to hubris and to abandon the lessons of history. What seems obvious today will very likely come off as risible tomorrow.

If we become humble, we will see the world as an often overwhelmingly complex place, filled with people on personal journeys to pursue happiness. We will be skeptical of calls to give the state power to do more than protect our rights to life, liberty, and the pursuit of happiness. As another humble philosopher, John Locke, put it, "Being all equal and independent, no one ought to harm another in his life, health, liberty, or possessions." Using violence to shape the lives of others in ways we prefer, but they do not, is anything but humble. Refraining from violence and resorting instead to voluntary persuasion is the humble—and libertarian—alternative.

Wisdom consists not only in realizing one's powers, but in realizing their limits.

9

AFRICA'S PROMISE
OF LIBERTY

By Olumayowa Okediran

Libertarianism in Africa is expanding and connecting with the indigenous African roots of liberty. The socialist mentality imported by Africa's former colonial masters, which identifies being "authentically African" with accepting the divisions among Africans along the lines of borders drawn up in Berlin, is finally being rejected. Africa's libertarians are working to unlock the potential of a modern, prosperous, and free Africa. Olumayowa Okediran is a member of the Executive Board of Students For Liberty, a founder of African Liberty Students Organization, and a student at the Federal University of Agriculture, Abeokuta, Nigeria.

Africa suffered from several colonialisms. There's the one we all know about, when various European and Arab states divided up and colonized the continent. That came to an end, more or less. (More in some places, and less in others.) Then there's the one that's ongoing. It's the colonialism of our minds. Many of the intellectuals here have been colonized by the ideologies of statism, which see markets as somehow anti-African, insist on using colonial borders to stop trade among Africans as preserving "African identity," and interpret our societies in the framework created by the German ideologue Karl Marx, who knew and cared nothing about our societies.

"Capitalism," by which they mean people creating goods and services for profit and trading them for other goods and services produced by others, is often branded as originating from the West and therefore alien to African culture. We hear the usual argument that capitalism inevitably results in the gradual disintegration of the social fabric, resulting in an ever-richer, but shrinking, "bourgeois" class to the detriment of the industrial workers and the peasantry. Marxist and Leninist thinkers emphasize that under a capitalist mode of production, that is, producing things for profit, the marginalization and immiseration of the peasantry is inevitable.

They never seem to ask, "Is it true?" Many European-trained African intellectuals come back with blinders on. They can't see their own societies anymore. They don't care to look into the histories of their own societies. They can't see what is before their eyes.

Scholars such as Professor George Ayittey have researched Africa's economic, social, and political past. What he and others have found would surprise the Marxists who insist that we Africans are not rational, that we don't understand trade, that we engage in primitive communist accumulation. What is the reality? We find a history of free trade in free markets, with prices set by consent between buyer and seller for mutual gain; entrepreneurship and innovation; long-distance trade; credit markets; firms and corporate management; and systems of commercial law.

Ayittey argues in his book *Defeating Dictators: Fighting Tyranny in Africa and Around the World*, that the economic system of Africa's ancient past holds some similarities to the "capitalism" that emerged in Europe and other regions, but it differed somewhat in structure. *The Merriam-Webster Dictionary* defines capitalism as an economic system characterized by private or *corporate* ownership of capital. African societies have always had that. As Ayittey explains,

> Peasants pool their resources together, cooperate, and help one another. This may be referred to as communalism or communitarianism, but it is not the same as

socialism or communism. One can be communalistic or socialistic without being a socialist. . . . Peasants go about their economic activities on their own free will, not at the behest of their tribal government. Communism involves state ownership of the means of production and, hence, all goods and services produced. But in peasant societies the means of production are owned by the clan, the lineage, which . . . acts as a corporate body or unit. However, the clan is not the same as the tribal government; it is a private entity and, therefore, the means of production are privately owned. Communal ownership is a myth.[61]

Family- or clan-owned farms or enterprises with the purpose of producing agricultural commodities for profit are capitalist activities. Ayittey argues that the communal nature of African societies has been grossly misinterpreted to imply that African societies are inherently socialist in nature. The limited liability joint-stock company we often associate with "capitalism" was a rather late introduction into European society.

Robert Hessen, the historian of corporate organization, showed that it's a myth "that limited liability explains why corporations were able to attract vast amounts of capital from nineteenth-century investors to carry out America's industrialization. In fact," he explained, "the industrial revolution was carried out chiefly by partnerships and unincorporated joint-stock companies, and rarely by corporations."[62] Family-owned businesses are common in many countries outside of Africa, as well. They are important drivers of production, exchange, and innovation in market economies everywhere.

Markets and trade have been an intrinsic part of African culture for millennia, as any student of African history knows. Ancient Africa is known for significant levels of trade that expanded dramatically from the seventh to the eleventh centuries, when trans-Saharan trade increased exponentially. The Mediterranean economies were in need of gold in exchange for salt, which meant big profit opportunities. Profit and entrepreneurship were the backbone of trade empires such as the Mali Empire, the Ghana Empire, and the Songhai Empire. Trade was the life of ancient African economies. The freely chosen activities of individuals—of farmers, blacksmiths, fishermen, market women, and professional merchants—were responsible for economic advancement; the anticipation of profit was the driving force behind those activities.

Were those activities the result of government planning? No. Markets evolved naturally as traders met at convenient places, often where two bush paths crossed. Peasant farmers and petty traders engaged in their respective businesses of their own volition with the aim of profiting, not to obey the orders of tribal or traditional governments.

There are variations among business forms around the world; the German corporation, the South Korean corporation, the Japanese corporation, and the American corporation each have their unique characteristics. So why should African businesses not also show variation? Family businesses are more important in Italy than in some other European countries. Just so in many African countries. But that doesn't mean that economic principles differ, or that communism, which did not work in Europe or China, would work in Africa.

Ayittey notes some differences between systems: "whereas an American individual may set out to start a business on his or her own, in Africa the extended family may do so." Profit from such ventures is shared by family members whereas under joint-stock capitalism, profit accrues to the primary entrepreneur, or in the case of a joint-stock company, to the shareholders. There are also differences in the scale of production. The ability to produce large quantities of services and goods leveraging on economies of scale is a characteristic of Western capitalism, whereas "the scale is brutally limited under peasant capitalism."[63]

Because of lawless and almost unlimited governments, one legacy of European colonialism and the continuing impact of statism, much economic activity is in the informal sector. Without the rule of law, it's quite difficult to make a living, but people do it. They rely, not on the state, which is often a failure, but on traditional African customary law. In the process, they have had to invest scarce resources to evade the kleptocratic state bureaucracies, the socialist state "marketing boards" (another legacy of colonialism that is now thankfully weakened or eliminated) that rulers used to oppress farmers and subsidize their supporters, and tariffs and trade restrictions.

The economic activities of the informal sector have contributed immensely to economic growth in Africa. The Expert Group on Informal Sector Statistics reported that the contribution of the informal sector (including the agricultural informal sector) to Sub-Saharan Africa's GDP is about 55 percent, a share that rises to 60 percent if Botswana and South Africa are included.[64] Profit, trade, and entrepreneurship are inherent aspects of indigenous economic systems in Africa.

A typical African city is a huge marketplace; a visit to Lagos in Nigeria exposes the enterprising nature of Nigerians; the city is a bustling hub of entrepreneurship. The sweating young man in the streets hawking ready-to-eat snacks, the young boy advertising cold bottles of table water, the bus conductor calling passengers to his vehicle, or the farmer in the nearby village going to till his melon farm with his family, these are the self-directed activities of individuals with the anticipation of profit. This is the Africa I know.

And they are the foundation of the Africa of the future, a continent of free people, freely trading, living peacefully. It is not the big international foreign aid bureaucracies, the former colonial masters (whether France or Britain), or the corrupt state monopolies and bureaucracies who will build our future. It is the market women. It is the African entrepreneur. It is what Professor Ayittey calls the Cheetah Generation, who reject corruption, embrace accountability, and who "aren't going to wait for governments to do things for them."[65]

Nigerian entrepreneur Tony Elumelu tells the story of an Africa with the potential to address its chronic economic and social challenges through private enterprise and entrepreneurship rather than through aid or government-to-government charity. He promotes what he calls Africapitalism: "The 'new' Africa: a reinvigorated private sector solving social problems by building businesses and creating social wealth. It is a drastic departure from the old model of centralised governments managing basic industries, a structure often developed at the recommendation of the well meaning but misguided global development finance institutions, supplemented by charity and foreign aid to target social issues."

In his manifesto, *Africapitalism: The Path to Economic Prosperity and Social Wealth*, Elumelu makes an unequivocal case for private enterprise and capitalism, encouraging "long-term, wealth-creating investments that build up communities, create opportunities to emerge from extreme poverty." Elumelu advocates market-based solutions to solving Africa's social problems and endorses free-market capitalism as the approach to "rebuilding and rebranding Africa as a land of investment, innovation, and entrepreneurship."[66]

I believe that to become prosperous, Africa must become more modern, but it does not follow that it must therefore become more "Western." Professor Olúfémi Táíwò, in his various writings, including his book *How Colonialism Preempted Modernity in Africa*, rejects "the tradition of placing Africans outside of the boundaries of common humanity." Modernity is not uniquely for Westerners or Europeans. Professor Táíwò argues that by understanding how "colonialism subverted modernity in the continent, we are enabled to make a stronger indictment of colonialism while simultaneously retrieving what is useful in the legacy of Africa's earlier transition to modernity that was aborted by the imposition of formal colonialism."[67]

It is important that we distinguish between modernization and westernization. The two phenomena are separate and separable. What can be considered modernization today is an evolution of interactions between civilizations—Africans, Americans (North, Central, and South), Asians, and Europeans. Protectionism and trade restrictionism cut Africans off, not only from other parts of the world, but from other Africans. There is nothing "authentically African" about clinging to the lines on the map drawn by European colonialists during the Berlin conference of 1884–1885. African intellectuals should reject absurd ideologies such as Marxism and do away with their hypocritical anti-Western tendencies and their laughable penchant for phony "authenticity." Africa should get on the modernization bandwagon and refuse to be placed "outside of the boundaries of common humanity."

Modernity means embracing the value of the individual human being. It means embracing production through voluntary cooperation and free exchange. It means embracing reason over superstition, law over force, production over plunder. It means embracing our own freedom and the freedom of each and every human being. As Professor Táíwò explained in *Africa Must Be Modern*, "We do not respect individuals because we love their choices or agree with them or even find them agreeable in the least. Indeed, we are required to respect them more so when we hate their choices and are repulsed by who they are or what they do. Respecting them for their sheer membership of the human species is what marks the modern age."[68]

Libertarianism in Africa is a growing force. It is not only the Cheetah Generation who will change Africa, but also those of my generation, who are still in college. We are impatient with corrupt, kleptocratic, and brutal governments. We insist on holding autocratic rulers to account. We applaud—and we demand—acceleration of the positive trend toward more accountable and constitutionally limited government, free markets, freedom of speech and press. We demand the responsibility and the liberty to run our own lives, to make our own choices, to pursue our own happiness. Libertarianism will change Africa for the better, and Africans will change the world for the better.

10

THE TANGLED DYNAMICS OF STATE INTERVENTIONISM: THE CASE OF HEALTH CARE

By Sloane Frost

Is state intervention and planning more rational, or does it yield merely "planned chaos"? The history of interventions into health care decisions and markets in the United States provides a useful case study into the dynamics of interventionism, which produce incoherent and irrational outcomes. Freedom of choice among competing options and providers of goods and services, although not planned at the aggregate level, provides more rationality and more plan coordination than interventionism. Sloane Frost is a director and co-founder of Students For Liberty and a research analyst with a public policy research firm based in Princeton, NJ. She received her master's degree in Public Policy and certificate in Health Administration Policy at the University of Chicago.

More than most of us know, our lives are directed, manipulated, even controlled by decisions made by politicians and bureaucrats. They can become so embedded in our lives that it can take an effort to notice them.

We know about the obvious cases, such as conscription (the draft), taxation, victimless crime laws, and the like. Usually those cases have some stated purpose behind them: force is used to intervene in our lives to get us to serve the state in war or in "civil service," or to get us to pay for projects or causes politicians support, or to get us to stop doing things politicians think are bad for us or condemned by their religion. But intervention isn't always so consciously contrived. It can grow, evolve, morph, until the whole system seems to take on a life of its own.

That's because interventions typically have unintended consequences. Controlling the price of milk may be intended to keep milk prices low, but the result is to create shortages of milk, which makes milk harder to find, causes long lines, fosters black markets and corruption, and makes the full cost consumers bear higher (price + waiting in line + bribes); those unintended consequences in turn often lead to calls for yet more intervention to fix the problems caused by the first intervention, and those secondary interventions may in turn yield additional problems that lead to calls for more interventions.

We get one intervention piled on top of another, with the bottom so far down hardly anyone remembers how the process started. The systems become embedded in daily life, as well, so much so that people never bother to ask how they got that way. What's worse, because they're not coherently planned, but lurch from crisis to crisis, they are sometimes described, not as state interventionism, but as "free markets" or "laissez faire" by people who don't take the time to understand the network of interventions and to trace out the incentives they create, how they affect behavior, and how they lead to unintended consequences and then more interventions.

One can't understand the international financial crisis if one doesn't pay attention to how a huge interlocking system of government interventions created a massive "housing bubble" in the US and how even more interventions into financial institutions induced banks to lower lending standards, generated mountains of debt, and spread the contagion globally by rating very risky debt as "risk free" or "low risk," encouraging financial institutions all over the world to purchase risky debt. No one planned to crash the economy, but the layers and layers of interventions had that effect, nonetheless. (The process is described in the contributions to *After the Welfare State*, an earlier book in this series.[69])

Interventionism vs. "Regulation"

Some people argue that because free markets are not subject to systemic planning by a central authority, they are less rational than government interventionism and control. After all, the market, unlike government, isn't planned. That assumes that government activities follow coherent, rational, and consistent plans. Experience shows that that's just not the case. Although government intervention is usually called "regulation," it's normally anything but. "Regulate" means "to make regular" and "to subject to a rule."[70] That's the original meaning of the term. Unfortunately, as the term was applied to government activity, it came over time to mean the opposite: "to intervene arbitrarily and capriciously"—and not only arbitrarily and capriciously, but in ways that are incoherent, irrational, and certainly not consciously planned.

The problem with interventionism ("a mutable policy") was foretold by James Madison, the principal author of the US Constitution, who wrote in *Federalist* No. 62,

> The internal effects of a mutable policy are still more calamitous. It poisons the blessing of liberty itself. It will be of little avail to the people, that the laws are made by men of their own choice, if the laws be so voluminous that they cannot be read, or so incoherent that they cannot be understood: if they be repealed or revised before they are promulgated, or undergo such incessant changes, that no man who knows what the law is to-day,

can guess what it will be to-morrow. Law is defined to be a rule of action; but how can that be a rule, which is little known, and less fixed?

Another effect of public instability is the unreasonable advantage it gives to the sagacious, the enterprising, and the moneyed few, over the industrious and uninformed mass of the people. Every new regulation concerning commerce or revenue, or in any manner affecting the value of the different species of property, presents a new harvest to those who watch the change, and can trace its consequences; a harvest, reared not by themselves, but by the toils and cares of the great body of their fellow-citizens. This is a state of things in which it may be said with some truth that laws are made for the few, not for the many.[71]

A system of interventionism, which can be changed by bureaucrats or politicians at their fancy, and in which "no man who knows what the law is today, can guess what it will be tomorrow," is decidedly *not* a system of regulation. (As Madison warned us, it is also the perfect occasion for what modern economists call "rent-seeking," the pursuit of private gain through control of the state. But that is not the main concern here.) The rule of law is what makes markets "regular"; interventionism does not. Piling one intervention onto another generates, not a coherent whole, but a system that fails to meet any coherent goals, is prone to periodic crises, and is, in effect, kept together with the legal equivalent of string, tape, and paperclips.

It helps to understand the dynamics of interventionism by examining a concrete case. A good case to study is state interventionism into one of the most important things we do together: taking care of our health and trying to help each other to live long and healthy lives. All over the world, decisions about health care are controlled, manipulated, forbidden, or mandated by state power. In some countries, the state has a monopoly over hospitals and professional medical care. In others it provides the bulk of the financing, through taxes levied on the population to finance payments to doctors and health care professionals. In most countries, doctors and nurses can only practice with permission of the state. The variety of interventionist systems is substantial. My field of both academic and professional work is studying US health care policy.

Health Care in the United States

Imagine you're a college student in the United States. Now imagine what happens when you get really sick. Your first thought may be about the homework you might be unable to finish, or maybe the party you'd miss, but if you feel really sick, you may think about seeing a doctor. Of course, that means that you'll have to determine what is covered by your insurance (if you've got insurance). If your symptoms worsen, you may decide to go to the emergency room (ER) or hospital and see a number of doctors, nurses, and administrative professionals. Though you may not realize it, your actions and choices were influenced by myriad health policies and regulations. That system grew over time. No one really designed it. To understand how your decisions about health and sickness are affected by government, let's look at it step by step.

One question you'll probably ask yourself when you get sick is what type of insurance you have. Health insurance companies operate by contracting with hospitals and providers to pay certain amounts in exchange for listing those hospitals and providers as options on the insurance plan. For example, if Dr. Nozick wants to be covered by Hayek Insurance, both parties will negotiate what rates Hayek Insurance will pay Dr. Nozick, whether per month, per patient, or per service rendered. In agreeing upon a package, Hayek Insurance will list Dr. Nozick as a provider in its network. When you then search for a doctor covered by Hayek Insurance, Dr. Nozick will be an option.

That process gets very complicated rather quickly. What accounts for the complications? Most Americans are insured through their employers, and many students are covered under a family plan. Why can't you simply buy an insurance plan that covers the doctor you want to see or services you think you may need? Why can't you shop online for health insurance like you can for car insurance? An enormous tangle of interventions rather severely limits your freedom of choice. No one planned the system; it follows a certain logic, but it's the logic of the incentives and crises created by interventionism.

During World War II, the US government imposed wage and price controls that prohibited employers from raising wages. In order to attract workers, employers turned to offering non-wage benefits, such as health insurance. In 1943 the "War Labor Board," whose members understood that the wage controls were causing problems in attracting workers to manufacture needed war materiel, ruled that the controls of the Stabilization Act of 1942 did not apply to insurance plans, so employers could offer what amounted to higher wages without violating the wage controls. In 1954 the Internal Revenue Service ruled definitively that insurance policies were not wages subject to taxation.[72] (After all, if it's not a violation of wage controls, it's not a wage, so it's not taxable.) You can imagine how people responded to those incentives. If a company offered you $1,000 to come and work for them, you would have to pay taxes on that additional income, so you wouldn't get the full benefit. But if they were to offer you a $1,000 insurance policy, it would be tax-free. Even after wage controls were abolished, there was still a big incentive to pay a part of wages in the form of insurance. People became accustomed to this benefit so much so that today we hardly question its existence or ask why we expect health insurance from our employers.

That system has since been codified. Some plans even allow you to save additional money in separate non-taxed accounts that can only be spent on health care-related purchases. If your income doesn't get taxed when put toward a state-sanctioned use, health insurance—as defined by the government—becomes in effect a subsidized purchase. Though employees may have preferred to get those dollars as wages to spend on a combination of other purchases, they are now encouraged to buy the company's health insurance instead. Moreover, thanks to a huge welter of interventions, the contents of plans are rather minutely dictated by a confusing array of government agencies.

The special tax treatment of wages offered as health insurance also means that businesses are encouraged by the government to negotiate on behalf of employees, and insurance companies negotiate with the business instead of with the employee. That indirect communication dictates that employees receive types of policies that they might not have chosen on their own. Employees are lumped in with their co-workers, rather than being allowed to purchase through other groups they might have preferred. Insurers have less incentive to negotiate with individuals or to offer customizable plans. All of that traps workers, a phenomenon known as "job lock." If they want to leave, they need to find another employer that offers insurance, since it is much more difficult to purchase on the individual market. Workers no longer choose to stay in a position because of job satisfaction or financial incentives. They also have to consider whether leaving a job will also leave them uninsured.

It gets more complicated. State governments also heavily intervene into insurance markets. Different states require plans to have different components. Those range from covering services such as pregnancy benefits, which not all women may wish to purchase,[73] to alcoholism treatment, mental health counseling, and more. Those are all fine things, but not every purchaser may be interested. That doesn't matter, because you and I are required to purchase them. Moreover, because different states impose very different minimum requirements, insurance companies must be licensed differently in each state. It is illegal for a person residing in New Jersey to buy a plan in Illinois, for example. Employers must offer plans in the state in which they are located, regardless of where their employees live. That means that an employer in New Jersey must offer a New Jersey plan, even if half its employees live across the river in Pennsylvania. It also means that markets become geographically restricted, which means less competition for insurers—and higher prices for you and me.

Getting back to what you do when you're sick, let's suppose that you do have a health insurance policy. Now you have to find a doctor. People in our generation usually do one of two things when we have a question like this: we look it up on a search engine or we post the question on a social networking site. Those options allow us to select based on reputation and feedback, which are especially important for something that involves as much trust as a health care provider.

But now you'll find that you don't have freedom of choice to choose your provider. Only certain people are allowed to treat you. Even if you just have an ear infection, only a licensed doctor can prescribe antibiotics to cure it. Even a nurse who has been practicing for twenty years and who attended three years of nursing school is legally prohibited from writing you a prescription. There are plenty of cases where you'd want more training than that—say, for brain surgery—but why can't a registered nurse (RN) write you a prescription when they can very easily look in your ear and see the classic signs of an ear infection? The reason is that our government does not let them. A doctor, who is more expensive and for whom you have to wait a longer time, must be the one to take fifteen seconds with a patient to write that prescription, even if he or she is just following the instructions given by the RN.

Now that the government has forced you to see Doctor Keynes when Nurse Sowell could have written the prescription, Doctor Keynes can charge you more money for his or her services because you don't have a choice. That came out of efforts by doctors to limit the competition; the restrictions they imposed also wiped out schools that trained black physicians and female physicians and greatly reduced the supply of doctors, which may explain why the American Medical Association was so enthusiastic about interventionism.[74] In fact, this practice can still be seen in licensing boards arguing over who may enter their guild or which accredited providers may perform services for which they are fully trained.

Even if you do find a doctor, however, you can't just go see any doctor. Since most doctors have contracted with a health insurance plan, they usually only take patients who are also insured by those plans. For example, if you want to see Dr. Ostrom, but she has an arrangement with Paterson Insurance instead of Hayek Insurance, she may not take you on as a new patient. Dr. Ostrom knows that she can be paid for services when she bills Hayek Insurance, but she runs the risk that Hayek Insurance doesn't cover things at the same rate, or makes her go through additional costly administrative procedures, or they pay too slowly or unreliably, or they just don't cover the procedure at all. Dr. Ostrom, therefore, prefers not to take any patients with Hayek Insurance. It's difficult as a provider to keep providing if she doesn't get paid.

Moreover, it's not easy to see a doctor if you don't have any insurance. Being uninsured may signal to the doctor that you are not employed and therefore less likely to be able to pay your bills. (Offering to pay 100 percent in cash on the spot does not ensure access, and it's not always so easy to secure treatment that way.[75]) You may not even be better off with government insurance, because that takes on average six months more than private insurance to pay the doctor, and even then, it's going to be at a much lower rate. Very few physicians are willing to wait in order to get paid a fraction of the bill.

Suppose you decide instead that you want to negotiate your own form of payment with the doctor. It seems reasonable enough, given that we write checks for large purchases ranging from computers to rent to tuition. The next time you see a doctor, you may even try this: ask the doctor how much a service costs. The vast majority of doctors will have no idea. Why? They don't need to know. No patient shops around at a doctor's office asking for how much procedures cost. There is no menu of prices, no visible way of evaluating or comparing doctors, even when it comes to common, everyday procedures.

And why should there be, when insurance covers everything? You as a patient are usually only responsible for paying the co-pay—the $20 or so that most insurance plans require when you visit a practitioner. Whether you see the doctor for five minutes or forty-five minutes, you will only pay that same $20 co-pay. It won't generally cost you more to get blood work done or an x-ray, if you get it done in the office. If you get an MRI or other non-invasive procedure, you still only have to pay $20 when you go to the office, even though the test itself may cost upwards of thousands of dollars. The price is a result of doctors and hospitals billing the insurance company with whom your employer has contracted, and they pay the rest of the bill.

All those interventions create some very imbalanced incentives. Doctors may prescribe tests that are unnecessary—and perhaps harmful—because patients have no reason to question them. We tend to assume that any test a doctor prescribes is necessary, but often they only order more tests to protect themselves from our litigious society. (Another government failure makes it virtually impossible to contract for risk, so doctors have to purchase hugely expensive malpractice insurance policies.) We may go see a specialist when an internist (a doctor who focuses on the entire body) can provide care that is just as high quality. We only pay $20 for that extra visit to a specialist, but that doctor may get a few hundred dollars for seeing us for just five minutes. Doctors may therefore overprescribe, and we don't question them.

In effect, all those interventions have transformed insurance into something that isn't really insurance anymore. The preferential tax treatment of employer-provided insurance has generated a distorted "third-party payer" system that amounts to a prepaid medical care plan. And that has helped to drive up medical prices substantially. Imagine that you had "food insurance" so that whenever you became hungry, you could go to a restaurant, have a meal, and have your insurance company (the "third party") pay the bill. What incentive would you have to resist that extra portion and what incentive would the waiter have to tell you the price of what you're ordering? Then, to control runaway prices, the insurance company has to scrutinize the bill, make deals in advance with certain restaurants and not others, and so on. Imagine what that would do to the food industry. Look at the medical industry for some hints about what to expect.

We complain about higher health insurance premiums for a very good reason. Premiums are a very complicated calculation, but one especially significant component of them is that insurance companies are required to cover a variety of services. For example, companies are required to reimburse for types of cancer screenings. Most of those services are only recommended if you are of a certain age or gender. Every time a service like that is added to the list of requirements, your premiums go up. Why? Because yet other interventions make it illegal for insurance companies to charge different amounts based on gender or certain other factors, such as age. That means that everyone, regardless of whether or not you use the service, has to pay. That may sound reasonable to many people as a way to help people pay for services they can't afford. But in the case of health insurance, everyone gets the subsidy equally. That means your subsidy as a young twenty-something may help cover a mammogram for a very wealthy sixty-year-old woman or treatments for a person who has been smoking and drinking heavily for his entire life. You cannot choose to purchase a different health insurance that does not cover those services—and therefore is more affordable—because companies are legally required to reimburse doctors and providers for those services. The government has effectively taxed you by raising your premiums and then delivered the subsidies indiscriminately. (And note that that kind of cross subsidization does not happen in the case of car insurance; lower-risk older drivers are not forced to subsidize the insurance premiums for higher-risk younger drivers.)

There is clearly a complex web of incentives at play in today's health insurance and health care systems. Most people don't think about them, but their lives are directed, manipulated, and controlled by a hodgepodge and incoherent system of interventions. They don't make the system more rational, but they do make it more difficult for us to make rational decisions about our own lives. We may want to balance quality, convenience, price, access, and reputation, but the interventions in place today prevent us from striking the right balance, that is, the right balance for us. Prices are increased thanks to prohibitions against interstate purchasing and the numerous services that insurance companies must cover, even if they are irrelevant to the individual buying a policy. Those and many other restrictions could be lifted without harming our health or our wallets. In fact, allowing people to buy insurance across state lines means companies would have to compete against each other and offer you better options.

A clear price system empowers us to fight against dysfunctional incentives and ensure that we are getting the care we need. Licensing laws restrict the supply of health care providers, meaning providers use the government to force us to purchase services from them, rather than from competing providers who could provide those services equally well at lower prices. Allowing competition in the provision of services and moving toward certification of skills, rather than limitation of supply, would increase the knowledge available to health care customers (condescendingly referred to as "patients" today) and would eliminate the absurdity that only certain people may prescribe antibiotics for even the simplest infections.

The medical system in the US is hardly the worst in the

world. It allows more freedom of choice than many and is where you want to be if you have insurance and a complicated condition. But the tangled web of interventions has generated a chaotic, incoherent, and crisis-prone system that costs more than it should (and would, if there were competition) and transforms us from active participants in our own health care choices into "patients," passive recipients of what the system delivers.

Health care technology has generated advances that our parents and grandparents could barely have dreamed of, but we won't reap the full benefits of that progress if we don't free ourselves from the system of state interventions that hem us in, restrict healthy competition, create webs of perverse incentives, and rob us of our dignity and of our freedom. We are responsible for controlling our future. We must therefore take back control of our own health. Healthy bodies are part and parcel of healthy lives, and liberty is the foundation on which we should build.

11

HOW DO YOU KNOW? KNOWLEDGE AND THE PRESUMPTION OF LIBERTY

By Lode Cossaer and Maarten Wegge

How can things known separately by millions of minds be made useful to each other? What advantages do free societies have over controlled or dictatorial societies in that regard? How do the rule of law, property, voluntary exchange, and prices solve problems that coercive central planning cannot solve? Maarten Wegge studied political science at ETH Zurich and at the University of Antwerp, where he received his master's degree, and was political officer of the Liberaal Vlaams StudentenVerbond (LVSV, Classical Liberal Flemish Students Association). He is currently academic director for the Murray Rothbard Institute in Belgium. Lode Cossaer received master's degrees in philosophy from the University of Antwerp and the Catholic University of Leuven and is currently working on a PhD proposal. He teaches economics in Brussels. Like Maarten Wegge, Cossaer was a political officer of the LVSV. He is an executive board member of the European Students For Liberty and president of the Murray Rothbard Institute in Belgium.

Suppose you were asked to make all the decisions for your own parents or siblings. Could you do that? Suppose you were asked to do the same thing for your friends and extended family? Do you think you'd be able to do that? Suppose that you had to make everyday decisions for billions of unknown strangers, both those alive today, as well as those who will live in the future. That would be quite the challenge, wouldn't it?

You'd need to know not only about facts, but about goals, as well. What goals should you seek to achieve? And after choosing the goals, how would you achieve them? F. A. Hayek referred to the set of problems involved as "the knowledge problem," which he characterized as "a problem of how to secure the best use of resources known to any of the members of society, for ends whose relative importance only these individuals know."[76]

In order to clarify what the knowledge problem is, we can divide it into three questions:

- First, how can a society optimize the use of knowledge?
- Second, how can we incentivize the use of knowledge in such a way that people would be induced to make their knowledge available to others?
- Third, how can we produce the knowledge needed for people to coordinate their actions and produce economic and social progress?

Those three questions lead to another, namely, what social processes are best suited to produce knowledge and to optimize and incentivize its use? The answer provided by liberals (or classical liberals or libertarians, depending on what linguistic tradition or country you're from) is what Adam Smith called "the obvious and simple system of natural liberty."[77] The central elements of such a system are "several property" (sometimes known as "private property") that is well defined, legally defendable, and transferable; freedom of exchange; and the rule of law to define, protect, and facilitate such free exchanges.

These issues pertain not merely to the most efficient way of organizing a society. They are also deeply rooted in morality and ethics. Would liberty be as important if all of us had perfect knowledge of what each and every one of us desired or needed, or of all of the facts known to each other? If such knowledge were possible, the argument for a centrally planned society might be more plausible, assuming, of course, that the planners were benevolent and publicly spirited. The simple fact, however, is that none of us is omniscient, even if we were all benevolent and public spirited.

Would you want someone else to decide everything on your behalf? Probably not. Each of us possesses intimate knowledge of our own personal goals and of the means available to us. Other people have a harder time accessing that specific knowledge. Other people rarely know as much about your situation as you do. And you rarely know as much about the lives of others as they do. There is a fundamental "asymmetry" when it comes to knowledge. That asymmetry is a good reason to endorse the presumption of liberty. One of the strongest arguments for liberty is based on understanding the knowledge problem.

Let's take a further look at what those insights mean for the emergence and sustainability of social order. By social order we mean a society in which we are able to coordinate our actions for mutual benefit, whether for play, production of wealth, or other purposes. What social order requires is what Hayek called "an order of actions." As Hayek noted, "What is required if the separate actions of the individuals are to result in an overall order is that they not only do not unnecessarily interfere with one another, but also that in those respects in which the success of the action of the individuals depends on some matching action by others, there will be at least a good chance that this correspondence will actually occur."[78]

Social *disorder*, on the other hand, implies human inter-action characterized by lots of crime, fraud, theft, assault, murder, or even war. Social order makes it possible for us to pursue our goals peacefully in voluntary cooperation with others, so we can devote our resources, not merely to bare survival (especially when pitted against others who are struggling to take from us our lives, our freedom, or our goods), but to the good things of life, such as friendship, love, creation, conversation, art, sports, discovery, invention, and the myriad other purposes of free people.

Institutions are what make such cooperation possible. Let's start by distinguishing between economic, political, and legal institutions.

Market Institutions: Exchange and Price

What kind of legal and economic order deals with the knowledge problem most effectively? What system of rules optimizes the use of knowledge? What system incentivizes people to make their knowledge available and useful to others? And what incentives lead to more knowledge, rather than less?

The system of natural liberty founded on property and freedom of contract fosters two seemingly incompatible forces: competition and social cooperation. We write "seemingly" because one need not choose one or the other. In a market, entrepreneurs, merchants, and firms compete with each other in order to earn the "custom" (or "business") of their customers, that is, to earn the chance to cooperate with them. The right to trade means also the right to choose with whom to trade, as well as the right to refuse to trade.

Property rights establish baselines; if you trade you exchange rights, and if you don't trade, you keep what is yours, so any voluntarily agreed exchange is an improvement over that baseline. Property rights also specify who has the freedom to decide what to do with a resource, subject to the normal rules against impinging on the freedom or harming the rights of others.

When the person with the freedom to decide what to do with a resource is also the person who can harvest its fruits and sell them, or benefit from its services, or sell the resource itself, that person has an incentive to take into account what others want and what others might do with the resource, because they can trade with him or her. That certainly doesn't mean that people don't make mistakes, but the ability to reap the reward of increasing the value of a scarce resource gives owners incentives to engage in those economic activities that create the goods and services consumers want to buy. And capital prices (the sale price of the resource) create for owners (and potential buyers) incentives to take the future into account, for a stream of future benefits is "capitalized" into a present price. (In technical terms, the price of a house is equal to the sum of all the future rents the house will yield, discounted by the rate of interest, which is a fancy way of saying that goods in the future can be valued now. If, however, capital prices cannot be established through voluntary exchange, because property and exchange are not allowed, then goods in the future won't have a present value and there will be little or no incentive to preserve; that is what is called in ecology "the tragedy of the commons."[79])

The mere act of buying and selling in a market creates prices, which communicate important knowledge: a price signals that someone, somewhere was willing to pay that specific price. It serves as a "proxy" for the alternative uses and valuations of a scarce resource. If I am deciding to make something, I can compare the prices of the various possible inputs that might go into it and those prices tell me what values other people put on them for other uses. I need to generate more value than those alternative values in order to sell the good for a profit; if I can only sell it for less than the sum of those values, then I take a loss, which is a rather effective way of informing me that I shouldn't keep on doing that.

Prices emerge from the decentralized acts of buying and selling—the "higgling and haggling"—that characterize markets. They emerge as the byproducts of acts of exchange and they transmit information very effectively in the universally understandable form of a number to all the actual—and potential—buyers and sellers of those goods. That's why there's no need for a central planning agency to produce some total aggregation of information in a market-based economy. Everyone in society who contributes to this process is a little island of knowledge, but their actions contribute to creating signals to guide the actions of others. Prices coordinate myriad individual plans and actions; by seeking their own profit, mutual benefits are generated and millions of people (each with access to limited bits of information and pursuing widely varied goals) can cooperate peacefully, offering to others their information, not only about their own goals, but about objective facts, technology, resource availability and more. That only happens if their pursuit of their own self-interest is restrained by everyone else's property rights, which are protected by the rule of law. If self-interest is combined with coercive power over others, then it will result instead in theft, violent conflict, and generally discoordination and disorder.

That's why both competition and social cooperation are processes, not perfect conditions of the market or society. Property, exchange, and prices provide incentives for us to reveal information to others in useful form and help us to coordinate our behavior without resorting to coercion or commands. It's certainly true that most (but not all) owners of firms resent competition from rivals, but those same people like it when *others* compete with each other to get his or her custom. We generally like lower prices for what we buy and higher prices for what we sell, so we like competition among those who produce and sell to us and resent people competing with us to sell what *we* produce. Overall, nonetheless, we're all a lot better off when free competition and free exchange are the rule. (The effort to secure monopolies, subsidies, and other special privileges through the coercive power of the state is known among economists by the somewhat confusing name of "rent seeking,"[80] and there are many studies of special-interest interventionist policies by "public choice" economists and political scientists.[81])

Free-market interaction is about creating value for people, not merely "maximizing profits."[82] Economic profit serves to tell us whether or not a company is actually adding value. A profit is the difference between what something is sold for and what it cost, with the costs expressed in money prices that tell us what other valued uses there are for the scarce resources used. And a loss, which is incurred when the good can only be sold for less than the cost of producing it, sends a rather effective signal that, rather than creating value, a firm or entrepreneur is destroying value. Profits and losses provide both information and incentives that coordinate behavior voluntarily and guide market participants to move resources to their most highly valued uses.

Political Institutions

How do political interactions compare to free-market interactions? What advantages or disadvantages does state action have in addressing the questions of knowledge we described in the introduction? Are there mechanisms by which institutions of political life—whether dictatorial or democratic, arbitrary or constitutional, unlimited or limited—optimize the issue of knowledge or incentivize people to produce knowledge or to reveal to others what they know? Are there analogues to profits and losses in the political sphere that allow us to judge political interactions in terms of success and failure, just as we rely on profits and losses in the economic sphere? Does political interaction—among politicians, bureaucrats, and the voting public—tell us enough about the wants and needs of others and provide incentives to meet them?

What distinguishes politics from other spheres of human interaction is that political interactions are based on coercion, rather than voluntary cooperation. Laws adopted by a majority in parliament are applicable to all of us, whether or not we agree with them. You are obliged to pay taxes whether you want to or not; not doing so can lead to seizure of your assets, loss of freedom by imprisonment, or worse. You have to "buy" what's offered to you, whether you chose it or not. And you get the whole package—foreign policy, tax policy, drug laws, marriage laws, schools, health care system, and on and on. You can't choose a little more of this and a little less of that, as you normally can in free-market transactions.

It's a bit like having to accept, in one gigantic take-it-or-leave-it transaction, a package that includes your house, your soap, your groceries, your phone, your eye glasses or contact lenses (even if you don't need or want them), your pets (even if you are allergic to them), your socks, and your collection of music, without being able to purchase any of those from other, competing providers, or merely to refrain from purchasing them. And because it's not voluntary, many (to say the least) of the transactions will not be mutually beneficial to all of those involved, whereas a market trade is between willing parties, and those not involved are protected by the rules of property from others who might wish to trespass on their rights.

Although people increasingly get a say in the running of government, due to the ever larger number of countries that are considered democracies, how much can voters convey to politicians about what they want or need? That is to say, what knowledge of our wants and needs can we communicate through the ballot? When we go out to vote, we are asked to communicate our preferences of so many things at the same time, it becomes difficult for anybody to make out why anyone voted this or that way, or what they want or need from their representatives. Politicians nowadays make decisions about taxation, diplomatic and military relations, the environment, education, spending on welfare, immigration, health issues, which products may or may not be bought and sold, housing, marriage—you name it and it's being voted on somewhere.

A voter might support a particular candidate because he or she agrees with that candidate on all of those issues, or because they care about one of them greatly and agree with the candidate on that particular issue. Voters might also choose the candidate they find trustworthy, knowledgeable, friendly, or even good looking. There is virtually no way of knowing the motivation of voters. And even if they say to pollsters, "I voted for candidate X because X seemed smart" (or "agreed with me on cutting [or raising] taxes," or "took a hard line against crime"), it's hard to know which of all the candidate's many other positions or characteristics they support or oppose. Voting for candidates is not an efficient way of discovering what voters think. (And it's made worse when you realize that one thing voters decide is whether others will be allowed to express their preferences or to live their lives as they wish; that's why unlimited democracy is sometimes described as two wolves and a sheep voting on what to have for dinner.)

If a business produces goods or services that people don't consider valuable, or that are too expensive for their budgets, the business makes losses and goes out of business. In contrast, governments can force us to pay for bad products and bad service, because they can use coercion. You may not like what governments produce, but you get it anyway. In a free market, consumers can buy goods or services that others don't want, and may even find terrible or distasteful. In free markets, purchasers can express their unusual tastes, so long as they don't harm others. When government provides goods or services, people generally have to settle for a one-size-fits-all product. You can't say you'd like a little less of that government activity and a little more of another. You get the package deal. We don't generally have the option when interacting politically to buy another product or switch to another provider of a service. We can't reveal our preferences about tradeoffs and choices "on the margin."[83]

Rule of Law
Rules are necessary for the existence of peaceful cooperation. Markets, no less than governments (and in many ways far more than governments) are governed by rules. As John Locke argued, "Where there is no law, there is no freedom."[84]

We can't just have people going about breaching contracts, stealing, aggressing against others, or generally violating rights. But rules need not be complex or complicated to work, or to undergird the order of a free society. Rather simple rules of property and contract generate prices that coordinate enormously complex forms of social order.[85] From the study of ecology to the study of flocks of birds and schools of fish, scientists have come in recent years to understand better how simple principles (or rules) can generate enormously complicated patterns. That's also true of human order: the simple rules of free societies generate more order and make possible more flourishing than the complex interventions of socialist planners.

To qualify as a "liberal" or "libertarian" framework for social order, certain formal characteristics (known generally as "the rule of law") are necessary: at the least, the rules should be clear and understandable; they should be impartially applied; and they should demarcate spheres of personal discretion within which one is free of arbitrary power or command.[86] All three are very important. Suppose that the rules in society are unclear, meaning they can be impossible (or excessively difficult) to understand, or retroactive, or even contradictory. That would mean that people wouldn't know in advance what is or isn't legal—what is or isn't subject to legal sanction. Among other faults, the uncertainty that comes with that kind of regime undermines planning, and thus the voluntary coordination of plans. The legal order should impart knowledge of the law and if it fails to do that, it fails to be a legal order at all.

Even clear laws require neutral judges. If a judge applies the rule in one way to members of one family and in another way to members of another family, it's not a rule. Or if the judge issues judgments because of bribes, or political pressure (what's called in some countries "telephone justice," meaning the judge gets a call from the "Ministry of Justice" telling him or her how to decide), or race, or religion, or language, or ethnicity, or some other reason other than the law and the facts of the case, it falls short of the rule of law. (That is not to say that the judicial function is mechanical; there is room for the exercise of practical wisdom, or what the Latins called *prudentia* and the Greeks *phronesis*, but such practical wisdom is not arbitrary or contrary to rules in the way that bribery, racism, or cronyism are.) Clarity of rules combined with a reasonable certainty that the rules will be enforced impartially go a long way to creating the framework for a just society.

But the legal order of a free society requires more than clear rules equitably applied. It requires that the laws define and protect spheres of discretion. A free person should, in the enjoyment of his or her life, liberty, and estate, not have "to be subject to the arbitrary Will of another, but freely follow his own," as Locke argued.[87] Everybody needs what Hayek called a "protected domain," within which she or he can make decisions. Without it, there would be little or no innovation, that is to say, little or no production of knowledge. Freedom isn't important merely because you get to do what you want to do; it's perhaps even more important because other people can do what they want to do. As Hayek explained, "What is important is not what freedom I personally would like to exercise but what freedom some person may need in order to do things beneficial to society. This freedom we can assure to the unknown person only by giving it to all."[88]

The knowledge problem also runs through all of the issues of law discussed above. It's rarely (if ever) obvious to all just what the right rule should be, nor its best interpretation or application. Those are important and complex issues. That is why thinkers in the classical liberal tradition have argued for decentralized mechanisms to identify good rules and public and transparent procedures of arriving at judgments. The former include such arrangements as local autonomy, federalism, and even competing and overlapping legal jurisdictions, so that mistakes can be corrected and superior practices discovered; the latter include public trials, publication of legal proceedings, open parliamentary discussion, freedom of the press, and other practices that secure transparency, so that corruption may be exposed, unfair proceedings revealed, and special interests unmasked. It's not enough to rely on good intentions or lofty justifications. A set of institutions suitable for a just and free society should be able to function even if bad people with wicked motivations intrude; it cannot depend on the purity of motives or the disinterestedness of actors, but should be able to survive not only the best cases (e.g., impartial, well-motivated, and reasonably well-informed governors), but also the worst cases (e.g., partial, power-hungry, and poorly informed governors). That is known as the condition of being "robust."[89] They should also be capable of adapting to circumstances, not merely resisting them; they should thrive on mistakes, as markets do (remember market competition is about "trial and error," and error is an important part of the learning that free markets facilitate). That has recently been dubbed "antifragile."[90]

Conclusion

Let's return to our opening questions:

- First, how can a society optimize the use of knowledge?
- Second, how can we incentivize the use of knowledge in such a way that people would be induced to make their knowledge available to others?
- Third, how can we produce the knowledge needed for people to coordinate their actions and produce economic and social progress?

Both the nature of the problem and historical experience suggest that top-down and coercive systems of command-and-control—the dream of socialists, fascists, National Socialists, International Socialists, and all other varieties of collectivist statists—don't work out so well. No person and no committee can have the information necessary to coordinate millions (or billions) of people with disparate goals and fragmentary knowledge. That's why liberty and the rule of law are so important. They do the job that central planning can't.

12

THE ORIGINS OF STATE AND GOVERNMENT

By Tom G. Palmer

Is the state responsible for wealth and social order? What is a state and what is a government? A short review of the sociology of the state shows that states emerged when "roving bandits" became "stationary bandits" and instituted regularized plunder. The achievement of liberty has been largely a product of subjecting states to law, a process that is still an ongoing struggle. (This essay was originally delivered as a lecture at the 2012 Cato University Summer Seminar.)

Many people believe that the state is responsible for everything. According to Cass Sunstein, a professor of law at Harvard University and former administrator of the White House Office of Information and Regulatory Affairs, "Government is 'implicated' in everything people own. . . . If rich people have a great deal of money, it is because the government furnishes a system in which they are entitled to have and keep that money."

That's the academic formulation of a concept that was restated recently in a popular form. "If you've been successful, you didn't get there on your own. . . . If you were successful, somebody along the line gave you some help. . . . Somebody helped to create this unbelievable American system that we have that allowed you to thrive. Somebody invested in roads and bridges. If you've got a business—you didn't build that.

Somebody else made that happen." That was Sunstein's boss, President Obama.

Even a charitable interpretation of the president's remarks shows that he doesn't understand the concept of marginal contribution to output, for example, of the value added by one additional hour of labor. He doesn't understand how wealth is produced.

Sunstein and his colleagues reason that since they attribute all wealth to the state, the state is entitled to it, and those who may foolishly think of themselves as producers have no claim of their own over it.

What exactly is a state? The canonical definition was offered by Max Weber, who defined the state as "that human community which (successfully) lays claim to the monopoly of legitimate physical violence within a certain territory."

In fact, it cannot be the case that all wealth is attributable to the state. Historically, the existence of a state apparatus required a pre-existing surplus to sustain it in the first place. The state, in other words, would not exist without wealth being produced before its emergence. Let's explore that a bit further.

Why do people have wealth? Charles Dunoyer, an early libertarian sociologist, explained that "there exist in the world only two great parties; that of those who prefer to live from the produce of their own labor and of their property, and that of those who prefer to live on the labor or the property of others." Simply put, makers produce wealth while takers appropriate it.

In his important book *The State*, the sociologist Franz Oppenheimer distinguished between what he called the economic means and the political means of attaining wealth, that is, between "work and robbery." "The state," he concluded, "is an organization of the political means."

The economic means must precede the political means. However, not all kinds of work produce surpluses sufficient for sustaining a state. You don't find states among hunter-gatherers, for instance, because they don't generate enough of a surplus to sustain a predatory class. The same is true of primitive agricultural societies. What is needed is settled agriculture, which generates a surplus sufficient to attract the attention of predators and sustain them. Such societies are typically conquered by nomads—especially those with horses, who were able to overpower sedentary agriculturalists. We see that happening over and over again after nomadic people erupted out of Central Asia long ago.

There is a memory of that ancient conflict preserved in the Book of Genesis, which tells the fratricidal story of Cain and Abel. It is significant that "Abel was a keeper of sheep, but Cain was a tiller of the ground," an echo of the conflict between settled agriculturalists and nomadic herders.

State formation represents a transformation from "roving bandits" to "stationary bandits." As the economist Mancur Olson wrote, "If the leader of a roving bandit gang who finds only slim pickings is strong enough to take hold of a given territory and to keep other bandits out, he can monopolize crime in that area—he can become a stationary bandit." That is an important insight into the development of human political associations.

The state is, at its core, a predatory institution. Yet, in some ways, it also represents an advance, even for those being plundered. When the choice is between roving bandits (who rob, fight, burn what they can't take, and then come back the following year) and stationary bandits (who settle down and plunder little by little throughout the year) the choice is clear. Stationary bandits are less likely to kill and destroy as they loot you and they fend off rival bandits. That is a kind of progress—even from the perspective of those being plundered.

States emerged as organizations for extracting surpluses from those who produced wealth. In his book, *The Art of Not Being Governed*, the anthropologist and political scientist James C. Scott of Yale University studies regions of the world that have never been successfully subdued by states. A central concept in his work is "the friction of power": power does not easily flow uphill. When waves of conquerors moved through an area, they subjugated the valleys, while those who escaped moved up into the less desirable highlands. Scott points out that those refugees developed social, legal, and religious institutions that make them very difficult to conquer. It's especially true of mountain people and swamp people. (It's a shame various leaders did not read Scott's book before occupying Afghanistan and promoting "state building" there.)

What are the incentives of the rulers? Overly simplistic models posit that rulers seek to maximize wealth, or gross domestic product. Scott, however, argues that the ruler's incentive is not to maximize the GDP, but to maximize the "SAP," the state-accessible product, understood as the production that is easy to identify, monitor, enumerate, and confiscate through taxation: "The ruler . . . maximizes the state-accessible product, if necessary, at the expense of the overall wealth of the realm and its subjects."

Consider (a ruler might say, "take"), for instance, agriculture. Rulers in Asia suppressed the cultivation of roots and tubers, "which has been anathema to all state-makers, traditional or modern," in favor of paddy rice cultivation. That is rather puzzling. Why would rulers care so much about what crops are planted? The reason, Scott notes, is that you can't very effectively tax plants that grow underground. Cultivators harvest them when they want; otherwise they remain in the ground. Paddy rice, on the other hand, has to be harvested at specific times by large concentrations of people, so it's easier for rulers both to monitor and tax the harvest and to draft the laborers into their armies. The incentives of rulers have systematic effects on many practices and permeate our societies.

State systems of social control—from military conscription to compulsory schooling—have thoroughly permeated our consciousness. Consider, for example, the passport. You cannot travel around the world today without a document issued by the state. In fact, you can no longer travel around the United States without a state-issued document. Passports are very recent inventions. For thousands of years, people went where they wanted without permission from the state. On my office wall is an advertisement from an old German magazine that shows a couple in a train compartment facing a border official demanding, "Your passport, please!" It explains how wonderful passports are because they give you the freedom of the world.

That, of course, is absurd. Passports restrict your freedom. You are not allowed to travel without permission, but we have become so saturated with the ideology of the state—and have internalized it so deeply—that many see the passport as conferring freedom, rather than restricting it. I was once asked after a lecture whether I favored state-issued birth certificates. After a moment, I said I could see no compelling reason for it and since other institutions can do it, the answer was "no." The questioner pounced! "How would you know who you are?" Even personal identity, it seems, is conferred by the state.

Modern states also claim to be the sole source of law. But historically, states mainly replaced customary law with imposed law. There is a great deal of law all around us that is not a product of the state, for law is a byproduct of voluntary interaction. As the great jurist Bruno Leoni argues, "Individuals make the law insofar as they make successful claims." Private persons making contracts are making law.

In the sixteenth century, the influential thinker Jean Bodin focused on the idea of sovereignty, which he defined as "the most high, absolute, and perpetual power over the citizens and subjects in a commonwealth." He contrasted that "indivisible power" with another kind of social order, known as customary law, which he dismissed because, he said, "Custom acquires its force little by little and by the common consent of all, or most, over many years, while law appears suddenly, and gets its strength from one person who has the power of commanding all." In other words, Bodin recognized that custom creates social order, but he *defined* law as requiring the hierarchical imposition of force, which in turn requires a sovereign—a power that is absolute, unconditioned, and therefore above the law.

That type of sovereignty is inherently contrary to the rule of law, as well as contrary to the principles of federal systems, such as that of the United States, in which power is divided among the different levels and branches of government. In constitutional regimes, the law, not absolute power, is held to be supreme.

The evolution of freedom has involved a long process of bringing power under law. The imposition of force has nonetheless left a powerful imprint on our minds. Alexander Rüstow, a prominent sociologist and a father of the post-war revival of liberty in Germany, meditated on the origins of the state in violence and predation and its lingering imprint: "All of us, without exception, carry this inherited poison within us, in the most varied and unexpected places and in the most diverse forms, often defying perception. All of us, collectively and individually, are accessories to this great sin of all time, this real original sin, a hereditary fault that can be excised and erased only with great difficulty and slowly, by an insight into pathology, by a will to recover, by the active remorse of all." It takes work to free our minds from our dependence on the state.

When meditating on what it means to live as free people we should never forget that the state doesn't grant to us our identities or our rights. The American Declaration of Independence states, "That to secure these rights, Governments have been instituted among men." We secure what is already ours. The state can add value when it helps us to do that, but rights and society are prior to the state. It's critical to remember that the next time someone says, "You didn't build that."

SUGGESTIONS FOR FURTHER READING

Liberty is not only an ideal of human interaction. It can also be used as a lens to examine and understand the world. Students will find readily available a huge and growing literature of liberty that draws on all of the social and moral sciences, on what used to be called the "humane sciences."

The lens of liberty helps us to notice things about the world that most people miss. One can come to see forms of order that others miss because they take them for granted; they don't focus on them because they lack the lens of liberty. People interact every day in complex ways without anyone issuing orders. The lens of liberty helps us to focus on the amazing world of spontaneous orders that surrounds us. It also helps us to see how violent intervention can disrupt such orders and replace "spontaneous order" with "planned chaos."

The lens of liberty can help us to see the dignity of people enjoying equal rights and the injustice and wrongness of violations of rights. It was the lens of liberty that helped people who had taken slavery for granted to see the evil and injustice of slavery; not to take it for granted as an eternal feature of the world, but to see it for the monstrous evil it was. The lens of liberty helps us to focus our attention on injustice and to focus our moral awareness on making a better, more just, more peaceful, and more prosperous world. In short: a world of equal liberty. It helps us to see how prosecuting crimes without victims fosters organized crime, corrupts law enforcement, and ruins lives.

There are many resources readily available to those who will seek them out. Here are some of the most useful:

Websites

Libertarianism.org offers a library of videos, essays, books, and other materials for anyone who wishes to explore libertarian ideas.

StudentsforLiberty.org provides articles, student-written blogs, and far more. It includes full-text versions, in PDFs that can be downloaded, of the earlier books in this series, including *The Economics of Freedom*, *The Morality of Capitalism*, and *After the Welfare State*.

Oll.libertyfund.org (the Online Library of Liberty) is not only a guide to blogs and other contemporary resources, but a gigantic library of the literature of liberty, including online versions of thousands of books, from the most popular to the most classical and scholarly.

Cato.org is produced by the Cato Institute, a leading libertarian research institute ("think tank"), and provides detailed studies applying libertarian principles and top-level research to particular issues of public policy—from taxation to marijuana prohibition to foreign and military policy to social security and medical policy. Cato maintains a special program for students at www.facebook.com/CatoOnCampus.

TheIHS.org is produced by the Institute for Humane Studies, which offers scholarships, seminars, and other valuable resources for students.

FEE.org is produced by the Foundation for Economic Education, one of the oldest libertarian think tanks in the US and the publisher of *The Freeman*. FEE organizes seminars for students.

IES-Europe.org is the website of the Institute of Economic Studies, Europe, which produces a wide range of seminars and other programs for European students.

LearnLiberty.org provides short, entertaining, and professionally produced instructional videos featuring classical liberal and libertarian professors.

AtlasNetwork.org provided by the Atlas Network, offers links to hundreds of groups and websites around the world for those who wish to explore the ideas of liberty in Russian, Arabic, Chinese, Spanish, Portuguese, Vietnamese, Lithuanian, Hindi, French, and dozens and dozens of other languages.

Books

In addition to the works footnoted in the essays of this book, the following recent books may be especially helpful for those who wish to go deeper into the ideas of liberty.

Libertarianism: A Primer, by David Boaz (New York: Free Press, 1998), integrates libertarian ideas across a wide range of topics in very clear language. (A new edition will appear in 2014.)

The Libertarian Reader, ed. by David Boaz (New York: Free Press, 1998), offers a wide range of classical and contemporary writings on libertarian themes.

Realizing Freedom: Libertarian Theory, Practice, and History, by Tom G. Palmer (Washington, DC: Cato Institute, 2009; new edition 2014), offers a range of essays, from the popular to the scholarly, that range over history, political theory, moral philosophy, economics, development, and more.

Robust Political Economy, by Mark Pennington (Cheltenham: Edward Elgar, 2011), draws on recent scholarship in public choice and provides a new approach to political economy that depends on realistic conditions to judge alternative systems of government.

The System of Liberty: Themes in the History of Classical Liberalism, by George H. Smith (Cambridge: Cambridge University Press, 2013), offers an approach to the ideas of liberty that is both very accessible and highly scholarly.

Free Market Fairness, by John Tomasi (Princeton: Princeton University Press, 2013), offers a somewhat technical treatment of issues in contemporary academic political philosophy and argues that free markets and limited government in reality satisfy the criteria of "social justice" better than state interventionism that seeks to mandate "socially just" outcomes.

About Tom G. Palmer

Dr. Tom G. Palmer is executive vice president for international programs at the Atlas Network. He oversees the work of teams working around the world to advance the principles of classical liberalism and works with a global network of think tanks and research institutes. Dr. Palmer is a senior fellow of the Cato Institute, where he was formerly vice president for international programs and director of the Center for the Promotion of Human Rights.

He was an H. B. Earhart Fellow at Hertford College, Oxford University, and a vice president of the Institute for Humane Studies at George Mason University. He is a member of the board of advisors of Students For Liberty. He has published reviews and articles on politics and morality in scholarly journals such as the *Harvard Journal of Law and Public Policy*, *Ethics*, *Critical Review*, and *Constitutional Political Economy*, as well as in publications such as *Slate*, the *Wall Street Journal*, the *New York Times*, *Die Welt*, *Al Hayat*, *Caixing*, the *Washington Post*, and *The Spectator* of London.

He received his BA in liberal arts from St. Johns College in Annapolis, Maryland; his MA in philosophy from The Catholic University of America, Washington, DC; and his doctorate in politics from Oxford University. His scholarship has been published in books from Princeton University Press, Cambridge University Press, Routledge, and other academic publishers. He is the author of *Realizing Freedom: Libertarian Theory, History, and Practice*, published in 2009; the editor of *The Morality of Capitalism*, published in 2011, and *After the Welfare State* published in 2012.

NOTES

Chapter 1

1   Jean-Jacques Rousseau, *The Social Contract*, trans. by Alan Cranston (New York: Penguin Books, 1968), p. 72.

2   Ibid., p. 64.

3   The full text of Spencer's memorable passage, from his essay "The Right to Ignore the State" is: "Perhaps it will be said that this consent is not a specific, but a general one, and that the citizen is understood to have assented to everything his representative may do, when he voted for him. But suppose he did not vote for him; and on the contrary did all in his power to get elected someone holding opposite views—what then? The reply will probably be that, by taking part in such an election, he tacitly agreed to abide by the decision of the majority. And how if he did not vote at all? Why then he cannot justly complain of any tax, seeing that he made no protest against its imposition. So, curiously enough, it seems that he gave his consent in whatever way he acted—whether he said yes, whether he said no, or whether he remained neuter! A rather awkward doctrine this. Here stands an unfortunate citizen who is asked if he will pay money for a certain proffered advantage; and whether he employs the only means of expressing his refusal or does not employ it, we are told that he practically agrees; if only the number of others who agree is greater than the number of those who dissent. And thus we are introduced to the novel principle that A's consent to a thing is not determined by what A says, but by what B may happen to say!" Herbert Spencer, *Social Statics: or,*

The Conditions essential to Happiness specified, and the First of them Developed, (London: John Chapman, 1851). Chapter: CHAPTER XIX: The Right to Ignore the State. Accessed from http://oll.libertyfund.org/title/273/6325 on 2013-03-23.

4   Joaquim Nabuco, *Abolitionism: The Brazilian Antislavery Struggle*, trans. and ed. by Robert Conrad (1883; Urbana, University of Illinois Press, 1977), p. 172. (In Conrad's translation, thus: "Let them educate their children—indeed, let them educate themselves—to enjoy the freedom of others without which their own liberty will be a chance gift of destiny. Let them acquire the knowledge that freedom is worth possessing, and let them attain the courage to defend it.")

5   John Locke, *The Second Treatise of Government*, in *Two Treatises of Government*, ed. by Peter Laslett (1690; Cambridge: Cambridge University Press, 1988), p. 306.

6   Michael Huemer, *The Problem of Political Authority* (New York: Palgrave Macmillan, 2013), p. 177.

7   Ibid., p. 178.

8   Ibid., p. 323. Locke located the root of property in general in each and every person's "Property in his own Person. This no Body has any Right to but himself." Ibid., p. 287.

9   Madison, James. 1983. "Property." In *The Papers of James Madison*, vol. 14: April 6, 1791–March 16, 1793. Charlottesville: University Press of Virginia. p. 266. The wider statement (available online at http://oll.libertyfund.org/title/875/63884) is: "This term in its particular application means 'that dominion which one man claims and exercises over the external

things of the world, in exclusion of every other individual.' In its larger and juster meaning, it embraces everything to which a man may attach a value and have a right; and *which leaves to every one else the like advantage.* In the former sense, a man's land, or merchandise, or money is called his property. In the latter sense, a man has a property in his opinions and the free communication of them. He has a property of particular value in his religious opinions, and in the profession and practice dictated by them. He has a property very dear to him in the safety and liberty of his person. He has an equal property in the free use of his faculties and free choice of the objects on which to employ them. In a word, as a man is said to have a right to his property, he may be equally said to have a property in his rights."

10   The data assembled over decades by the researchers at the Fraser Institute of Canada in the annual *Economic Freedom of the World Report* and made publicly available at www.freetheworld.com show clearly that more freedom produces better results everywhere, whether Europe or Asia, Africa or Latin America.

11   Richard Epstein, *Simple Rules for a Complex World* (Cambridge, Mass: Harvard University Press, 1995).

12   The science of economics emerged hundreds of years ago when people began to notice that countries that had freer markets tended to be more orderly and prosperous and that the king's ministers were not needed to coordinate supply and demand. As the historian Joyce Appleby noted, "Economic writers had discovered the underlying regularity in free market activity. Where moralists had long urged that necessity knows no law, the economic analysts who pursued price back to demand had discovered a lawfulness in necessity, and in doing

so they had come upon a possibility and a reality. The reality was that individuals making decisions about their own persons and property were the determiners of price in the market. The possibility was that the economic rationalism of market participants could supply the order to the economy formerly secured through authority." Joyce Appleby, *Economic Thought and Ideology in Seventeenth-Century England* (Princeton, N.J.: Princeton University Press, 1978), pp. 187–88.

Chapter 2

13   John Emerich Edward Dalberg, Lord Acton, *Historical Essays and Studies*, by John Emerich Edward Dalberg-Acton, edited by John Neville Figgis and Reginald Vere Laurence (London: Macmillan, 1907). Chapter: APPENDIX, Letter to Bishop Creighton, accessed from http://oll.libertyfund.org/title/2201/203934 on 2013-05-19.

14   For the case of American voters, see David Boaz, David Kirby, and Emily Eakins, *The Libertarian Vote: Swing Voters, Tea Parties, and the Fiscally Conservative, Socially Liberal Center* (Washington, DC: Cato Institute, 2012).

15   "An Introduction to Libertarian Thought," video at www.libertarianism.org/introduction .

16   Fareed Zakaria, "The 20 Percent Philosophy," *Public Interest* 129 (Fall 1997), pp. 96–101, cited in Tom G. Palmer, "Classical Liberalism and Civil Society," in *Realizing Freedom: Libertarian Theory, History, and Practice* (Washington, DC: Cato Institute, 2009), p. 221.

17   "Sharon Statement," available at http://en.wikipedia.org/wiki/Sharon_Statement .

18   Barry Goldwater's 1964 Acceptance Speech, available at www.washingtonpost.com/wp-srv/politics/daily/may98/goldwaterspeech.htm.

19   Port Huron Statement, available at http://en.wikipedia.org/wiki/Port_Huron_Statement.

20   Carl Oglesby, *Ravens in the Storm, A Personal History of the 1960s Anti-War Movement* (New York: Scribner, 2008), p. 120.

21   Carl Oglesby, *ibid,* p. 173.

22   Milton Friedman, "It's Time to End the War on Drugs," available at www.hoover.org/publications/hoover-digest/article/7837; Jeffrey A Miron and Jeffrey Zwiebel, "The Economic Case Against Drug Prohibition," *Journal of Economic Perspectives,* Vol. 9, No. 4 (Fall 1995), pp. 175–192.

23   Lysander Spooner, *Vices Are Not Crimes: A Vindication of Moral Liberty*, available at http://lysanderspooner.org/node/46.

24   An array of law enforcement officials who are willing to speak out on the disasters of prohibition can be found at Law Enforcement Against Prohibition, http://www.leap.cc.

Chapter 3

25   For an extended treatment of these issues, I very highly recommend George H. Smith, *The System of Liberty: Themes in the History of Classical Liberalism* (Cambridge: Cambridge University Press, 2013).

26   Joseph Schumpter, *History of Economic Analysis* (New York: Oxford University Press, 1974), p. 394.

27   I deal at much greater length with the emergence and growth of civil society in my essay "Classical Liberalism and Civil Society: Definitions, History, and Relations," in *Civil Society and Government*, ed. by Nancy L. Rosenblum and Robert C. Post (Princeton: Princeton University Press, 2002), pp. 48–78, reprinted in Tom G. Palmer, *Realizing Freedom: Libertarian Theory, History, and Practice* (Washington, DC: Cato Institute, 2009).

28   Henri Pirenne notes that "The burghers were essentially a group of *homines pacis*—men of peace." *Medieval Cities: Their Origins and the Revival of Trade.* Princeton: Princeton University Press, 1969), p. 200.

29   Henri Pirenne, *Economic and Social History of Medieval Europe* (New York: Harcourt Brace Jovanovich, 1937), p. 50. In European languages two terms emerged to describe these new social orders: *burgenses* and *civitas*. "The expression burgenses was at first used only if the city was not a civitas, and civitas was at first only the old episcopal seat ('Bischofsstadt')." Hans Planitz, *Die Deutsche Stadt im Mittelalter: Von der Römerzeit bis zu den Zünftkämpfen* (Graz, Austria, and Köln, Germany: Böhlau, 1954), p. 100. *Burgensis* and *bürgerlich* enter English via French as "bourgeois." Later the derivatives of the terms—bürgerlich/bourgeois and civil—came to be used interchangeably. ("Burg" persisted in English in such names as Hillsborough and Pittsburgh, and in the name of the oldest representative assembly in English colonies, the House of Burgesses.)

30   See Brian M. Downing, *The Military Revolution and Political Change* (Princeton: Princeton University Press,

1992) and Charles Tilly, *Coercion, Capital, and European States* (Oxford: Blackwell, 1992).

31   See Hendrik Spruyt, *The Sovereign State and Its Competitors* (Princeton: Princeton University Press, 1994).

32   "The Trew Law of Free Monarchies," King James VI and I, *Political Writings*, ed. by Johann P. Sommerville (Cambridge: Cambridge University Press, 1994), p. 75.

33   Adam Smith, in his famous book published in 1776, *An Inquiry into the Nature and Causes of the Wealth of Nations*, not only addressed what *causes* "the wealth of nations," but also what its *nature* is. "The wealth of nations" isn't the wealth of the ruling elite, or the court, or the gold in the king's treasury. "According therefore, as this produce, or what is purchased with it, bears a greater or smaller proportion to the number of those who are to consume it, the nation will be better or worse supplied with all the necessaries and conveniences for which it has occasion." Adam Smith, *An Inquiry into the Nature and Causes of the Wealth of Nations*, vol. I, ed. R. H. Campbell and A. S. Skinner (Indianapolis: Liberty Fund, 1981), p. 10. Thus, Smith identified the wealth of nations, not with the wealth of the court, but with the annual produce of the combined labor power of the nation, divided by the number of consumers, a conception that persists in the modern notion of per capita gross domestic product. He stated the causes of the wealth of nations in a lecture: "Little else is requisite to carry a state to the highest degree of opulence from the lowest barbarism, but peace, easy taxes, and a tolerable administration of justice; all the rest being brought about by the natural course of things. All governments which thwart this natural course, which force things into another channel, or which endeavour to arrest the progress of

society at a particular point, are unnatural, and to support themselves are obliged to be oppressive and tyrannical." Quoted by Dugald Stewart from a now lost manuscript in Stewart's "Account of the Life and Writings of Adam Smith, LLD," in Adam Smith, *Essays on Philosophical Subjects*, ed. W. P. D. Wightman and J. C. Bryce, vol. 3 of the *Glasgow Edition of the Works and Correspondence of Adam Smith* (Indianapolis: Liberty Fund, 1982), p. 322.

34 See *The English Levellers*, ed. by Andrew Sharp (Cambridge: Cambridge University Press, 1998).

35 E. L. Godkin, "The Eclipse of Liberalism," *The Nation*, August 9, 1900, reprinted in David Boaz, ed., *The Libertarian Reader* (New York: The Free Press, 1997), pp. 324–326, p. 326. Godkin's diagnosis of the cause of liberalism's decline deserves attention: "To the principles and precepts of Liberalism the prodigious material progress of the age was largely due. Freed from the vexatious meddling of governments, men devoted themselves to their natural task, the bettering of their condition, with the wonderful results which surround us. But it now seems that its material comfort has blinded the eyes of the present generation to the cause which made it possible. In the politics of the world, Liberalism is a declining, almost a defunct force."

36 Some of the most important recent studies of the mass murder and enslavement carried out by Communist and National Socialist (Nazi) regimes include Anne Applebaum, *Gulag: A History* (New York: Random House, 2003), Timothy Snyder, *Bloodlands: Europe Between Hitler and Stalin* (New York: Basic Books, 2010), and Frank Dikötter, *Mao's Great Famine, The History of China's Most Devastating Catastrophe, 1958–1962* (New York: Walker & Co., 2010).

37   Much of that story is colorfully told, from an American perspective, by Brian Doherty in *Radicals for Capitalism: A Freewheeling History of the Modern American Libertarian Movement* (New York: Public Affairs, 2007).

38   Robert Nozick, *Anarchy, State, and Utopia* (New York: Basic Books, 1974), p. ix.

39   Francisco de Vitoria, "On the American Indians," *Political Writings*, ed. by Anthony Pagden and Jeremy Lawrance (Cambridge: Cambridge University Press, 1991), pp. 250–251.

40   Quoted in Perez Zagorin, *How the Idea of Religious Toleration Came to the West* (Princeton: Princeton University Press, 2003), p. 119.

41   John Milton, "Areopagitica: A Speech of Mr. John Milton for the Liberty of Unlicenc'd Printing, to the Parliament of England" [1644], in *Areopagitica and Other Political Writings of John Milton* (Indianapolis: Liberty Fund, 1999), p. 23. John Locke later argued in his famous letter on toleration, "[I]t is one thing to persuade, another to command; one thing to press with arguments, another with penalties." John Locke, "A Letter on Toleration," in *The Sacred Rights of Conscience*, ed. by Daniel L. Dreisbach and Mark David Hall (Indianapolis: Liberty Fund, 2009), p. 47.

42   In his Elegy to Gournay after his death, his friend and student Anne-Robert-Jacques Turgot noted that Gournay understood the folly of imposing monopolies and "standards" on the market that consumers did not, in fact, demand. As Turgot put it, Gournay "was astonished to see that a citizen could neither make nor sell anything without having bought the right to do so at

a great expense in a corporation," that is, that one had to first purchase from a monopolistic guild the right to undertake a trade and offer goods to willing customers. "He was far from imagining that this piece of stuff, for not being conformable to certain regulations, might be cut up into fragments of three ells length, and that the unfortunate man who had made it must be condemned to pay a penalty, enough to bring him and his family to beggary." Turgot, "Éloge de Gournay," in *Western Liberalism: A History in Documents from Locke to Croce*, ed. by E. K. Bramsted and K. J. Melhuish (London: Longman, 1978), p. 305.

43 James Buchanan, "Order Defined in the Process of Its Emergence: A note stimulated by reading Norman Barry, 'The Tradition of Spontaneous Order,'" *Literature of Liberty*, v. 5, n. 4 (1982) Accessed from http://oll.libertyfund.org/title/1305/100453 on 2013-03-23.

44 Some libertarians believe that a constitutional order without a monopolization of law or the use of defensive force, that is, without a state, is both possible and desirable. See, for examples, Randy E. Barnett, *The Structure of Liberty: Justice and the Rule of Law* (Oxford: Oxford University Press, 2000), Michael Huemer, *The Problem of Political Authority*, *op. cit.*, Bruce L. Benson, *The Enterprise of Law: Justice Without the State* (Oakland: Independent Institute, 2011). My own quite brief statement of "The Case for Ordered Liberty Without States" can be found at http://www.libertarianism.org/publications/essays/case-ordered-liberty-without-states. Whether liberty can be enjoyed without a state is disputed among libertarians, but the mere non-existence of the state is not the same as the enjoyment of liberty, for liberty depends crucially on institutions of law and justice. The question on which

there is not general agreement is whether law and justice can exist without a monopolistic provider.

Chapter 4

45 I contrast the principle of liberty with a principle of "equality of outcomes" rather than a principle of "equality" because the principle of liberty is already a principle of "equal liberty."

46 St. Thomas Aquinas, "Treatise on Law, Q. 96, Art. 2," *Summa Theologica* (Westminster, Maryland: Christian Classics, 1981), p. 1018.

Chapter 5

47 Agelina Grimke, "Slavery and the Boston Riot," *The Liberator*, 12 August 1837.

48 Orlando Patterson, *Slavery and Social Death: A Comparative Study*, (Cambridge: Harvard University Press, 1982), vii.

49 For the Enlightenment's contribution to the concepts of individual liberty and natural rights, see M. Zafirovski, *The Enlightenment and Its Effects on Modern Society*, (New York: Springer, 2011), particular page 40 which notes: "No doubt, individual liberties and choices, civil rights, a private sphere or privacy, personal autonomy, fulfillment, well-being, humane life, and happiness are firmly established and taken for granted values and institutions in modern Western democratic and other societies, particularly, but not only America. . . . If so, then they are first and foremost the product and legacy of the Enlightenment and its liberal-secular individualism."

50   Frederick Douglass, "What to the Slave is the Fourth of July?" 5 July 1852; L. M. Child, *An Appeal in Favor of that Class of Americans Called Africans,* 1833.

51   Mary Wollstonecraft, *A Vindication of the Rights of Woman,* 1792, in Mary Wollstonecraft, *A Vindication of the Rights of Men* and *A Vindication of the Rights of Woman*, ed. by Sylvana Tomaselli (Cambridge: Cambridge University Press, 1995), p. 74.

52   Declaration of Sentiments and Resolutions, Seneca Falls Convention, 1848. http://ecssba.rutgers.edu/docs/ seneca.html. Accessed 18 February 2013.

53   Frederick Douglass, "West India Emancipation Address," 3 August 1857.

54   Declaration of Sentiments.

55   Richard Cobden, *Speeches on Questions of Public Policy by Richard Cobden,* ed. by J. E. T. Rogers, www.econlib.org/ library/YPDBooks/Cobden/cbdSPP14.html. Accessed 22 February 2013.

56   James G. Birney, *A Letter on the Political Obligations of Abolitionists, with a Reply by William Lloyd Garrison* (Boston: Dow and Jackson, 1839), p. 32.

57   W. Phillips, "Philosophy of the Abolition Movement" (1853), *Speeches, Lectures, and Letters* (Boston: Lee and Shepard, 1884), p. 113.

58   L. Menand, *The Metaphysical Club: A Story of Ideas in America,* (New York: Farrar, Sraus, Giroux, 2001), p. 13.

59   B. Dylan, "The Times They Are A-Changin'," Columbia Records, 1964.

60   W. L. Garrison, *The Liberator*, 31 January 1831.

Chapter 8

61   George B. N. Ayittey, *Defeating Dictators: Fighting Tyranny in Africa and Around the World* (New York: Palgrave Macmillan, 2011), p. 43.

62   Robert Hessen. "Corporations," *The Concise Encyclopedia of Economics*. 2008. Library of Economics and Liberty. Retrieved 19 May 2013, from www.econlib.org/library/Enc/Corporations.html.

63   George B. N. Ayittey, ibid., p. 76.

64   Jacques Charmes, "Measurement of the Contribution of Informal Sector and Informal Employment to GDP in Developing Countries: Some Conceptual and Methodological Issues," available at www.unescap.org/stat/isie/reference materials/National-Accounts/Measurement-Contribution-GDP-Concept-Delhi-Group.pdf.

65   See Professor George B. N. Ayittey's TED presentation, www.ted.com/talks/george_ayittey_on_cheetahs_vs_hippos.html.

66   Tony O. Elumelu, *Africapitalism: The Path to Economic Prosperity and Social Wealth*, www.tonyelumelufoundation.org/sites/tonyelumelufoundation.org/files/Africapitalism%20White%20Paper%20FINAL.pdf.

67 Olúfémi Táíwò *How Colonialism Preempted Modernity in Africa* (Bloomington: Indiana University Press, 2010), p. 48.

68 Olúfémi Táíwò, *Africa Must Be Modern* (Ibadan, Nigeria: Bookcraft 2011), p. 48.

Chapter 9

69 *After the Welfare State*, ed. by Tom G. Palmer (Ottawa, IL: Jameson Books, 2012). See especially the essays on "The Tragedy of the Welfare State" by Tom G. Palmer and "How the Right to 'Affordable Housing' Created the Bubble that Crashed the World Economy" by Johan Norberg.

70 See the treatment of the history of the term in Randy E. Barnett, "The Original Meaning of the Commerce Clause," 68 *University of Chicago Law Review* 101 (2001), available at www.bu.edu/rbarnett/Original.htm and Randy E. Barnett, "New Evidence on the Original Meaning of the Commerce Clause," 55 *Arkansas Law Review* 847 (2003), available at http://randybarnett.com/55ark847.html.

71 James Madison, in George W. Carey, *The Federalist* (The Gideon Edition). Edited with an Introduction, Reader's Guide, Constitutional Cross-reference, Index, and Glossary by George W. Carey and James McClellan (Indianapolis: Liberty Fund, 2001). Chapter: No. 62: Concerning the constitution of the senate, with regard to the qualifications of the members; the manner of appointing them; the equality of representation; the number of the senators, and the duration of their appointments Accessed from http://oll.libertyfund.org/title/788/108681 on 17 May 2013.

72　See Laura A. Scofea, "The Development and Growth of Employer-Provided Health Insurance," *Monthly Labor Review*, March 1994, available at www.bls.gov/mlr/1994/03/art1full.pdf and Thomas C. Buchmueller and Alan C. Monheit, "Employer-Sponsored Health Insurance and the Promise of Insurance Reform," NBER Working Paper 14839, available at www.nber.org/papers/w14839.pdf.

73　See Circular Letter No. 23 (1976), "Re: Mandatory Maternity Coverage," "The law specifically requires maternity care coverage be provided in "Every policy..." without any restrictions based on age, sex or marital status," available at www.dfs.ny.gov/insurance/circltr/1976/cl1976_23.htm.

74　The awful story is told in great detail in the classic article by Reuben Kessel, "The A.M.A. and the Supply of Physicians," 35 *Law and Contemporary Problems* (Spring 1970), available at http://scholarship.law.duke.edu/cgi/viewcontent.cgi?article=3288&context=lcp&sei-redir=1.

75　Paying in cash is not always a legal transaction. Doctors who accept Medicare may not collect cash for the Medicare-covered service. Brent R. Asplin, MD, MPH; Karin V. Rhodes, MD; Helen Levy, PhD; Nicole Lurie, MD, MSPH; A. Lauren Crain, PhD; Bradley P. Carlin, PhD; Arthur L. Kellermann, MD, MPH, "Insurance Status and Access to Urgent Ambulatory Care Follow-up Appointments," *Journal of the American Medical Association*, September 14, 2005, http://jama.jamanetwork.com/article.aspx?articleid=201518.

Chapter 10

76   Friedrich A. Hayek, "The Use of Knowledge in Society." *American Economic Review*. XXXV, No. 4. pp. 519–30. American Economic Association. 1945. Library of Economics and Liberty [Online] available from www. econlib.org/library/Essays/hykKnw1.html; accessed 12 May 2013; Internet. See also Thomas Sowell, *Knowledge and Decisions* (New York: Basic Books, 1996).

77   Adam Smith, *An Inquiry into the Nature and Causes of the Wealth of Nations*. Edwin Cannan, ed. London: Methuen & Co., Ltd. 1904. Library of Economics and Liberty [Online] available from www.econlib.org/library/Smith/smWN19.html; accessed 12 May 2013.

78   F. A. Hayek, *Law, Legislation, and Liberty: Volume I, Rules and Order* (Chicago: University of Chicago Press, 1973), pp. 98–99.

79   www.econlib.org/library/Enc/TragedyoftheCommons.html

80   www.econlib.org/library/Enc/RentSeeking.html

81   www.econlib.org/library/Enc/PublicChoice.html

82   For more explanation and evidence, see the essays in *The Morality of Capitalism*, ed. by Tom G. Palmer (Ottawa, IL: Jameson Books, 2011), especially "Interview with an Entrepreneur" (interviewing Whole Foods Market co-founder John Mackey) and "The Paradox of Morality," by the Chinese libertarian scholar Mao Yushi.

83   For good introductions to the scientific study of choices in politics, see *Public Choice: A Primer*, by Eamonn

Butler (London: Institute of Economic Affairs, 2012) and *Government Failure: A Primer in Public Choice*, by Gordon Tullock, Gordon Brady, and Arthur Seldon (Washington, DC: Cato Institute, 2002).

84 John Locke, *Second Treatise of Government*, chapter VI, section 57.

85 See Richard Epstein, *Simple Rules for a Complex World* (Cambridge, MA: Harvard University Press, 1995).

86 The classical liberal legal scholar Lon Fuller identified eight ways that one can fail to make law in his book *The Morality of Law* (New Haven: Yale University Press, 1939), pp. 33–37. Hayek expanded further: "The law will consist of purpose-independent rules which govern the conduct of individuals towards each other, are intended to apply to an unknown number of further instances, and by defining a protected domain of each, enable an order of actions to form itself wherein the individuals can make feasible plans." F. A. Hayek, *Law, Legislation, and Liberty: Volume I, Rules and Order* (Chicago: University of Chicago Press, 1973), pp. 85–86.

87 John Locke, *Second Treatise of Government*, chapter VI, section 57.

88 F. A. Hayek, *The Constitution of Liberty*, ed. by Ronald Hamowy (Chicago: University of Chicago Press, 2011).

89 See for discussions of robustness P. J. Boettke and P. T. Leeson, "Liberalism, Socialism, and Robust Political Economy," in *Journal of Markets & Morality* (2004), 7:1, pp. 99–111 and Mark Pennington, *Robust Political Economy: Classical Liberalism and the Future of Public Policy* (Cheltenham: Edward Elgar Publishing, 2011).

90 See Nassim Nicholas Taleb, *Antifragile: Things that Gain from Disorder* (New York: Random House, 2012).

INDEX

Liberty at your Fingertips

CATO
INSTITUTE

Support Students For Liberty

Students For Liberty is an international libertarian advocacy and education organization dedicated to providing a unified, student-driven forum of support for students and student organizations dedicated to liberty. To that end, Students For Liberty strives to identify, develop, and empower talented young people who are interested in the ideas of individual liberty, free-market capitalism, limited government, and restrained foreign policy.

What began as a single event at Columbia University in 2008 with only 100 attendees has become what Whole Foods, Inc. co-founder and CEO John Mackey now describes as "the premier pro-liberty student organization." Since its founding, SFL has built a network of over 50,000 students, connecting over 900 pro-liberty groups on college campuses all over the world. SFL hosts dozens of regional conferences for thousands of students annually, distributes free resources all over the world—including 350,000 copies of *Why Liberty*—and hosts rigorous leadership training programs. Its reputation and continuous growth led Edward H. Crane, founder of the Cato Institute—the most prominent libertarian think tank in the world—to describe SFL as "critical to the future of liberty."

In order to maintain its independence, Students For Liberty accepts no government funding. Support for SFL's programs and initiatives comes from generous contributions from individual donors, in addition to contributions from foundations and corporations. SFL is a nonprofit, tax-exempt, educational foundation under Section 501(c)3 of the Internal Revenue Code.

Students For Liberty
1101 17th Street, N.W., Suite 810
Washington, D.C. 20036
www.studentsforliberty.org

A Free Academy, A Free Society

Students For Liberty is a network of pro-liberty students from every corner of the globe. We work to educate our fellow students on the ideas of individual, economic, and academic freedom.

 Find out more at:
www.studentsforliberty.org

 Find us on Facebook:
facebook.com/studentsforliberty

 Follow us on Twitter:
@sfliberty

Students For Liberty provides resources for pro-liberty students and student groups, including:

Dozens of Regional Conferences Each Fall
Free Books
Annual International Students For Liberty Conference
Tabling and Activism Kits
Academic Webinar Series
Academic Symposia
Leadership Handbooks and Training
...And Much More!

Find out more about our resources and **join the student movement for liberty** at:

www.studentsforliberty.org

Free Markets Need a Moral Defense: *Yours*

The Atlas Network has initiated a worldwide moral campaign for free enterprise, starting with honest debates about morality and capitalism in many languages. Atlas has partnered with Students For Liberty to promote serious discussion and debate about the morality of the free market to bring you: *The Economics of Freedom, The Morality of Capitalism, After the Welfare State,* and *Why Liberty,* edited by Atlas Executive Vice President Dr. Tom G. Palmer. Atlas also sponsors books, essay contests, webinars, web platforms, and Freedom Schools in over a dozen other languages, with the generous support of the Smith Family Foundation and other sponsors.

- The Atlas Network consists of more than 450 independent, free-market think tanks and organizations that are based in the U.S. and in more than 80 countries.

- Atlas organizes training programs, regional conferences, and many other programs to identify and empower institutions and intellectual entrepreneurs who believe in liberty.

- If you'd like to become involved, visit AtlasNetwork.org and check out our worldwide directory, our Resource Library and other online tools.

ATLAS
N E T W O R K

Atlas Economic Research Foundation
1201 L St. NW • Washington, DC 20005 • 202-449-8449
AtlasNetwork.org

Enroll Today! The Atlas Leadership Academy

Whether you're thinking of starting your own organization, an associate at a think tank, a director of development, or an executive director, the Atlas Leadership Academy provides the opportunities you need to advance your cause. The Atlas Leadership Academy is a flexible, credit-based curriculum that allows you to gain the skills needed to succeed in the free-market think tank world.

This program provides:

- Training on classical liberal values

- A six-week course to help you determine how you can contribute to the cause of liberty

- Introductory and advanced think tank management courses (both online and live)

- Specialized online skills training.

We know that your scarcest resource is your time, and these programs allow you to gain these skills on *your* schedule, when it's convenient and useful for you. Atlas caters to a worldwide network of free-market leaders, and now, anyone can have access to our exciting products and training.

**Claim your first credit by enrolling in the
Atlas Leadership Academy today at
AtlasNetwork.org/ALA.**

"This Book Can Change Your Life!"

Young people today are being robbed—of their rights, of their freedom, of their dignity, of their futures. The culprit? The "progressive" ideology now taught in too many universities, an ideology which created a world-straddling engine of theft, degradation, manipulation, and social control. This path-breaking book defines the problem and offers America's youth a path to the future—before it is too late.

Please consider giving copies of *Why Liberty* to students and teachers, local political leaders, business and labor associations, the news media, and to your activist friends all across America. Knowledge is power in political debate. This book will give you that power.

Special Bulk Copy Discount Schedule

1 book	$ 9.95	25 books	$ 85.00	500 books	$1,250.00
5 books	$25.00	50 books	$150.00	1000 books	$2,000.00
10 books	$40.00	100 books	$275.00		

All prices include postage and handling.